Library Solutions Institute #2
Duke University, June '93

Cartoon by librarian-cartoonist Gary Handman, author of
Bibliotoons: A Mischievous Meander Through the Stacks and Beyond
(Jefferson, NC: McFarland, 1990) and countless other laughter-making
drawings spotted regularly in *American Libraries* and *Wilson Library
Bulletin*. This drawing was on T-shirts given to each Institute participant.

RETHINKING REFERENCE

IN ACADEMIC LIBRARIES

THE PROCEEDINGS AND PROCESS OF
LIBRARY SOLUTIONS INSTITUTE NO. 2

UNIVERSITY OF CALIFORNIA, BERKELEY
MARCH 12-14, 1993

DUKE UNIVERSITY
JUNE 4-6, 1993

LOUELLA WETHERBEE • INSTITUTE FACILITATOR

ANNE GRODZINS LIPOW • EDITOR

LIBRARY SOLUTIONS PRESS • BERKELEY, CALIFORNIA

RETHINKING REFERENCE
IN ACADEMIC LIBRARIES

First printing
October 1993

Book design by
Catherine Dinnean

LIBRARY SOLUTIONS PRESS

Sales Office
1100 Industrial Road, Suite 9
San Carlos, CA 94070
Fax orders: 415-594-0411

Editorial Office
2137 Oregon Street
Berkeley, CA 94705
Telephone: 510-841-2636

ISBN 1-882208-02-1
Printed in the United States of America

CONTENTS

Frontispiece: cartoon by Gary Handman

PREFACE • *Anne G. Lipow*

Why This Program?
How This Book is Organized
About the Organizers
Acknowledgements
About Library Solutions Institutes

PART 1: THE PROCEEDINGS

PART III: APPENDICES

PREFACE
WHY THIS PROGRAM; WHY THIS BOOK

Anne G. Lipow

Director, Library Solutions Institute
Berkeley, California

If you have been working in a library in the 1990s, you have by now accepted—whether enthusiastically, reluctantly, or fearfully—the notion that libraries must undergo fundamental changes if they are to survive in the coming century. When you think about what the future might hold, you anticipate that there will be new types of jobs, different services, different tools to work with, new looks to library organizational structure. You have certainly experienced the signs: technology that diminishes the need for miles of shelved books; that collapses space and time, making irrelevant where the information resides in relation to the person who wants it or the time of day it is wanted. You know that information seekers are increasingly learning about library information resources from sources other than the library, sources that are handier to them than the library. You are suspicious of the ability of these non-library sources to do a proper job of pointing the information seeker toward relevant materials, but since these sources also speedily deliver the requested information, you contemplate how your library could provide that level of convenience. Aware of evolving software that analyzes text and, in effect, catalogs and classifies it, you wonder what effect that will have on traditional library jobs. You have also experienced budget cutbacks that severely reduce library collections and staffing. It occurs to you that perhaps there is a message in the shutting down of library schools. If closings continue, where will the new library professionals come from? How are the existing schools changing their curricula to meet the new times? You are even prepared to go with the advice you read in the professional literature: flatten the library's hierarchical organization; drop traditional services and invent new ones, retool yourself to acquire the necessary skills; look at the positive side of diminishing budgets.

However, it is one thing to understand and accept that change is inevitable, and quite another to know what to do to participate in it constructively. With all of our foresight, there is a shortage of ideas about what steps to take now to ensure our relevance among the next generation of information providers. Within library administrations, the kind of leadership that effectively steered large library staffs in more stable times is not sufficient in these times. Today's leaders require more than a smart vision. They also must have the ability to inspire confidence and willingness to follow among people who don't want to undergo change.

A typical attempt today at moving toward change seems to go something like this: library administrators look to their staff for help ("What can you stop doing so we can make room to meet new demands?"). Library staff, without the tools to comply, respond defensively ("Hey, that level of decision is YOUR job!") or, if something is offered up on the sacrificial altar ("Let's stop serving our secondary clientele"), likely as not, it is rejected as too extreme to fly. Also, pressure to change is coming from the outside: from the parent organizations to which libraries report, from library users, and from competing information providers. We could stand an infusion of creative, practical ideas that librarians at all levels believe they could make work.

And so, with the goal of raising some new questions and penetrating new ideas, under the auspices of Library Solutions Institute, and with the cooperation of The Library of the University of California, Berkeley, the first of the "Rethinking Reference" institutes was organized. It was clear that the entire library needed to be rethought, but experience dictated that we start small and where visible results were likely. Why pick reference? Two reasons. First, reference hadn't undergone a period of major upheaval as had other library departments, and might be more amenable to new ideas. Catalog, acquisitions, ILL, and circulation departments each had made it through significant reorganization and restructuring of jobs, and key staff in those departments might be feeling protected from the pressure to undergo more change, thinking that they'd had their turn. Second, change in a reference department, with its direct relationship with library users, surely had to call into question all other functions within the library. Unlike the other library departments that managed to accomplish their reorganization with little effect on the definition of the library system as a whole, if reference departments needed to serve patrons differently, the rest of the library – the hidden support to library users – would need to rethink how it did business. So start with reference, and it wouldn't stop there.

Within a few weeks after the Berkeley Institute was announced, enrollment was filled. A second Institute was organized, this time on the east coast, at Duke University. That, too, filled within weeks. As of this writing, a third is scheduled, to be held in Iowa. The demand goes on, but given the Institute requirement that enrollment not exceed 60 (for maximum individual participation), it is greater than can be met in a timely way.

Therefore, these proceedings: to share the papers of the Institute with those who could not attend.* Therefore, too, the section on "process," which is intended to give a leg up to those who wish to organize rethinking sessions in their local libraries or regions. That is, the ideas *per se* that were generated at the Institute may be less important than the participants' movement forward to new positions of readiness to take action and to work with their colleagues back home toward major change. In a sense, the Institute was a quasi-training session in creative envisioning and strategizing. If spending a bit of time practicing thinking beyond the borders of our experience will help libraries and librarianship move foreword with imagination, leadership, and speed, we hope this book helps to encourage the flowering of such activity.

September 1993

---

* Audio tapes of the formal presentations at the Berkeley institute are also available (see information at the back of this book), and may provide a perspective different from what you'll get by reading those same presentations. In four cassettes, they include the audience discussion that followed each speaker (not included in this book). Also, hearing the speeches—with the speakers' emphasis on particular words, their pacing, their side remarks—may call your attention to passages and ideas you glossed over or interpreted differently in reading them.

How This Book Is Organized

Part I covers the goings on at the two Institutes. In Part II the organizers discuss the key considerations in their design of the program and describe the major steps in its preparation. The Appendix includes program-related documents.

About the Organizers of the "Rethinking Reference" Institutes

Anne G. Lipow is founder and director of the Library Solutions Institute. She is co-author of *Crossing the Internet Threshold: an Instructional Handbook* (Berkeley, CA: Library Solutions Press, 1993). She consults, speaks, writes, and instructs in areas of organizational change, staff skills development, and issues about use and teaching of electronic resources. She has worked with libraries of all types throughout the U.S., as well as in Australia, New Zealand, Hong Kong and Germany. Among the library skills workshops she presents are "Neutral Questioning," "Making Effective Presentations," "Teaching Library Electronic Resources," "Customer Service Skills," "Job Training Skills," and "Outreach programs to targeted constituencies". Formerly she was Director of Instructional Services at the University of California,Berkeley, Library.

Lou Wetherbee is a consultant to libraries in the U.S. and Latin America. Her expertise spans a wide range of issues related to managing libraries in an environment of technological change: directing complex planning processes, group facilitation, personnel selection, conflict resolution, and technology policy planning. She has considerable experience in the design and organization of cooperative library services and library network governance, resource sharing, electronic publishing, and networked information. Based in Dallas, Texas, she is a frequent seminar and conference speaker in the area of emerging technologies for libraries and library networking.

ACKNOWLEDGEMENTS

I am indebted to Andrea Spurgeon and Jenny Lipow for greatly improving the manuscript. Under hectic conditions they clarified confusing passages, corrected errors in grammar, and caught inconsistencies in format. Aiming for timeliness over perfection, I take full responsibility for any remaining errors or unclear wordings.

My appreciation and admiration goes to each of the contributors to this book. I have learned mountains from every one. Special thanks go to the following:

- Kenneth Berger, Johannah Sherrer, Rich Hines, Karen Williams, and James Rettig for their willingness to continue the "BI debate" in written form (see Aftermath: The Future of Bibliographic Instruction: An Unresolved Issue)

- Janice Koyama and Johannah Sherrer for permission to reproduce their homework assignments (see Appendix A: Starting the Institute before the Scheduled Date)

- Bill Whitson and Ann Pettingill for permission to reproduce their post-Institute memos to their colleagues (see Aftermath: Sharing Experiences with Colleagues)

- Alfred Willis and Eugene Matysek for permission to reprint their article "Place and functionality of reference services from the perspective of TQM theory." (see Appendix B: Selected Readings)

- Jeffrey Michaels for permission to reproduce his bibliography "Vision and Strategic Planning" (see Appendix B: Selected Readings)

Finally, it goes without saying that this book would not have been possible without the 125 participants in the Institutes. Collectively and individually, they deserve a special applause.

Editor

ABOUT LIBRARY SOLUTIONS INSTITUTES

Library Solutions Institutes provide a forum for structured learning and discussion among small groups of up to 60 participants who wish to grapple with issues in librarianship that have no easy answers. The aim is to arm the participants with skills and ideas that enable them to contribute significantly to the shaping of the profession.

LSI #1, "Crossing the Internet Threshold," teaches participants Internet skills as a foundation for planning strategies for reorganizing the library environment to meet new demands and options for the storage, retrieval, and delivery of information. The instructors are nationally recognized Internet experts and advisors in the application of Internet tools within libraries.

LSI #2, "Rethinking Reference: New Models and How to Get There" addresses issues of change in reference services required by user needs, technological innovations, and budget reductions. The faculty are acknowledged leaders in the profession in areas of library administration, education, and reference services. Versions of this program have been presented throughout the United States and in several cities in Australia.

PART I: THE PROCEEDINGS

1 • IN SEARCH OF NEW FOUNDATIONS FOR REFERENCE

Jerry D. Campbell
Keynote Speaker
University Librarian, Duke University

I think it was one hot Tuesday in August of 1991 when the letter arrived. I mean, of course, the letter that got me into all this trouble over reference. The letter was innocent enough in appearance – official "CAL POLY" stationary with logo in that relaxing shade of forest green. Like an unsuspecting fool, I opened and read it.

> As the editor of Reference Services Review, *I am writing to invite you to submit a manuscript on changing economic models for reference service. This topic was discussed at a recent editorial board meeting, and complements the paper you recently presented at the ALA conference in Atlanta (staff vs. collections).*

The letter went on to say, "As the sister publication to Library Hi Tech, we are also interested in the affects of technology on the provision of reference service, and effectively managing for these continual changes."

Needless to say, I was somewhat taken aback at being asked to propose a new economic model for reference. Not since the early 1980's had I been known for my involvement in reference issues, and even then it wasn't anything I wanted to remember, since it recalled the unfortunate situation in which I assumed directorship of a library that had absolutely no reference librarians and more than a little need for them. I might yet have escaped if the author of the letter, Ilene Rockman, had not included her e-mail address. The ensuing e-mail communications virtually sealed my fate. Editor Rockman indicated that it would be acceptable, no, that it would be preferable if I would propose something that would be provocative, something that would stimulate a vigorous discussion of reference issues among reference librarians. Well, I might not be an expert in matters of reference, but hardly anyone can claim to provoke librarians more than I. Indeed, being constructively provocative for the sake

My point is...to emphasize the importance of achieving conceptual clarity early in the search for new models.

of helping librarians face the challenges of a changing information world has somehow become my role within the profession. After studying the matter for a couple of months, I agreed to take the assignment, though I did give Editor Rockman the opportunity to reconsider. I wrote, "I have had some great 'no-holds-barred' sessions with my reference colleagues and am beginning to have some strange ideas. Are you sure you don't want to back out on publishing an article like this?" She held firm.

For the record, Editor Rockman told me at the ALA Mid Winter meeting in Denver that the resulting essay had met their goal of engendering discussion and debate—even though I, for my trouble, had been burned in effigy with some fiery words on at least two list-serves.

I have given this brief introduction both to let you know what possessed me to venture into this reference "territory" and to set a tone for not taking ourselves too seriously. Sometimes when dealing with an extremely important subject as we are here, it helps us to add a little humor and have fun. I hope we can also be bold and take some intellectual risks in this search for new reference models.

THE NEED FOR CONCEPTUAL CLARITY

Now let me turn my remarks to the effort to shake the foundations and find a new model for reference. First, I want you to understand that the most important thesis of the essay "Shaking the Conceptual Foundations of Reference: A Perspective" (hereafter, "Shaking") is that reference librarians need to achieve some conceptual clarity about their evolving mission and role in the context of the changing knowledge environment. As you may recall from the essay, I am fundamentally dissatisfied with the notion prepared by the ALA Standards and Guidelines Committee that information service can be defined as "personal assistance provided to users and potential users of information." I realize that it is arguably unfair of me to criticize this statement on the basis of being a poor mission statement since it was only intended to provide guidelines for providers. Yet, how can guidelines be drawn if it is not clear what those guidelines demarcate? In my opinion, personal assistance to users and potential users of information is not your mission, but is rather merely one activity that is required by your mission. In any case, acknowledging and focusing on the task of developing conceptual clarity with regard to the mission and role of reference librarians is considerably more important than debating the merits (or demerits) of the specific recommendations of my 1992 essay.

4

Viewed in this light, the major difficulty of that essay was my decision not to include the simple mission statement that lay behind my depiction of the newly christened access engineer. I did, in fact, write one. The closest I came to stating it was in the section defining and describing access engineering, and therein lies the reason that I chose such an infelicitous phrase to name the new-age reference librarian. Let me recall for you key parts of that description:

> *Access Engineering: We must become much more adept at transferring information upon demand from its source directly to the user. So the third and final task of our new Access Engineers is to actually engineer this transfer. The new Access Engineers, therefore, must play the central role in information transfer...[T]hey should actually take the lead in envisioning and engineering the design of new information delivery technology to reach out to the end-user...They should also assume a leadership role in reforming or creating alternatives for our existing access mechanisms like circulation, interlibrary loan, and so on, which require in-building use.*

The mission statement I worked from was this: **It is the mission of access engineers to design, develop, and operate methods of delivering library and other information on demand to users wherever they may be.** If this is a sound mission statement, then all the other functions I listed for the access engineer, namely, making sense of the myriad of sources of information (knowledge cartography), finding out what information our consumers of information want (consumer analysis), and playing the central role in information transfer (access engineering), are required by it and should flow from it. Even the research and development function I described in the economic modeling section was derived from this mission statement.

My point is not just to make this mission statement explicit, but also to emphasize the importance of achieving conceptual clarity early in the search for new models. If we begin with a clear sense of mission, it is much easier to define new roles and construct new models because the mission itself will help generate requirements and set boundaries. It keeps us from wasting our energy on functions that are outside its bounds. And of equal importance, a clear mission statement will help us measure how well we are doing along the way when we attempt to execute a new model. It provides a benchmark for gauging progress.

Conversely, if we do not develop clarity about the reference mission, we may find it very difficult to agree on what we should or should not do. This sort of reminds me of another country song: "There ain't nothin' wrong, there just ain't nothin' right!" By way of confession, let me indicate the reason that I decided to exclude the mission statement from my essay. Its absence made it necessary for the serious reader to think through the essay carefully in order to figure out its implications for the mission of reference librarians. And I viewed the task of making librarians think about reference to be part of my assignment. It is harder for the reader to understand and evaluate a new model, however, if its cornerstone remains veiled. For this reason, were I to begin again, I would include it. We may find ourselves developing a set of guidelines with nothing more at its core than personal service, which is a style of providing service but hardly a mission. Perhaps you can see why I was distressed to find no discussion of a reference model, not to mention the mission that lies behind it, when I began work on my RSR assignment. Conceptual clarity is crucial.

THE NEED FOR DATA

Second to my concern for conceptual clarity is my interest in compiling real, usable data about the practice of reference. Even if we ascertain what the operative mission for reference as we know it is, and even if we agree to make no changes in it, without more data it will be hard for us to improve how well we carry it out.

You will recall that in preparing to write the essay, "Shaking," I wished to discover in some detail what reference librarians did. More particularly, I hoped to learn more about the questions they answer. There was a purpose in my search. Knowing more about the questions not only could tell me what reference librarians are doing but also could provide me with important keys to their mission from the inside out, so to speak. As a fringe benefit, it could help in identifying problem areas in our library and wider campus information environment.

You will recall that in the absence of real data, I substituted some hastily developed categories and estimated the percentage of questions they represented and the amount of staff time they required. That was my only recourse if I wished to make even the most gross generalizations about where we might apply technology and to what effect. I hope that in the meantime some of you will have begun to collect real data. For purposes of our deliberations here, let me share with you one more formal means to collect such data that we have been experimenting with at Duke, namely, a cause/effect diagram.

Presuming that the effect is a question, Figure 1 represents one means of developing a list of the causes behind the questions. In this early example of our efforts, we chose six rather broad and inclusive categories that would allow virtually any cause to be placed on the diagram. Other categories can be added if necessary. The purpose of the cause/effect diagram is merely to give us a tool to identify as accurately and comprehensively as possible what causes the questions that come to the reference desk. Such diagrams can be done individually or in groups; groups are best because of the free-wheeling, free-associating that usually results.

The information from such diagrams can subsequently be rendered into one or more checklists for keeping records as questions are asked. If such checklists are used periodically to sample the causes behind the questions, they will soon render valuable information not presently available from any other source. For instance, you may discover that a considerable number of questions can be prevented by solving certain problems of library origin, such as confusing arrangements and lack of signage. It may make concrete with real data what you have already suspected. You may even find that it is at least part of the mission of reference to clean up after other ineffective library operations. More importantly, however, you will begin to develop a detailed picture to reveal with some precision what lies behind the questions. Such data will help you begin to think in terms of missions and models.

Let's take this example of data collecting one step further. After keeping the checklists for a time, suppose we total the questions and compare them both by category and sub-category. The results might look something like this:

From this simple pareto chart in Figure 2, a chart for comparing relative volume, we can quickly see the level of demand placed on reference by various causes. In this somewhat hypothetical example, we can see that the people category (in this case a category for research/knowledge questions) accounts for most of the questions. We would, of course, hope this was the case. We would not, however, be amused that environmental factors accounted for such a large portion of the business (in this case about 28%). If 28% of the demand for reference is generated by a poor environment, then we should improve the environment and let reference librarians get on about some new, more substantial business.

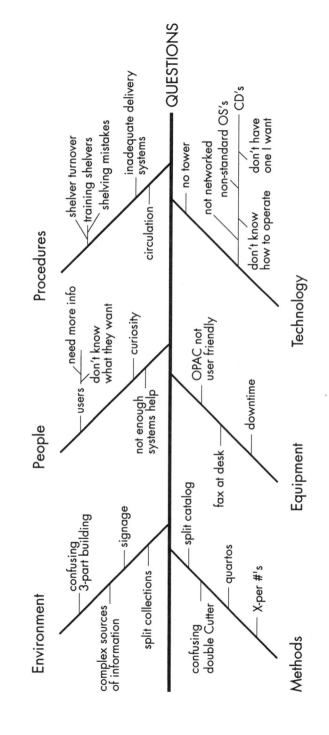

Figure 1 Causes of Reference Questions

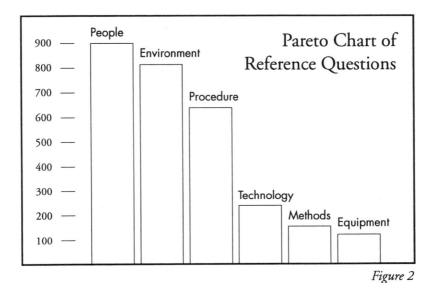

Figure 2

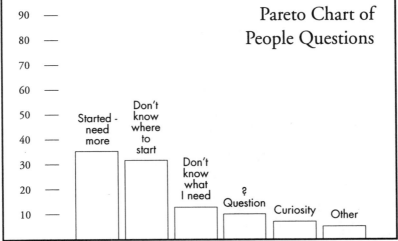

Figure 3

For diagnostic purposes, we can also put the items in an individual category on a pareto chart (Figure 3). This gives us even finer detail about a specific category. In this example, I've used the largest source of questions from Figure 2, questions which come from people's lack of knowledge. Even this unrefined example begins to suggest fundamental solutions that might prove to be useful alternatives to the more passive reference model currently in use.

But again, my point is only to reinforce my earlier plea in the essay on "shaking the foundations" for collecting real data about our current reference practices. Such data will be essential to understanding the current practice and developing useful new models for the future.

KNOWING WHAT THE USER WANTS AND NEEDS

The third point I want to emphasize concerns the matter of consumer analysis. Our lack of knowledge about how our users would prefer to get information is not just a reference problem. All librarians have been accustomed to serving up information on our terms and expecting our users to meet those terms. When we have asked them about their opinions, we have customarily set the boundaries within our existing practices, that is, we have limited their responses by the choices we allow. We must truly begin to understand the changing desires of our users as they relate to acquiring knowledge and information.

This is particularly important during this generation because of the changes underway and the differences of opinion about the changes. Most of us serve complex user groups that represent a range of viewpoints. Some hate the presence of computers and all it represents in libraries. For others, we cannot change to an electronic environment fast enough. In evolving the new library environment, we must be keenly aware of the dimensions of these conflicting viewpoints and the many viewpoints that fall somewhere in between. If user satisfaction is important (and I believe it is), then we must seek a course that serves the largest possible number of our constituents and alienates as few as possible. We cannot afford to

> All librarians have been accustomed to serving up information on our terms and expecting our users to meet those terms. . . We must truly begin to understand the changing desires of our users as they relate to acquiring knowledge and information.

change our libraries too quickly for our audiences, nor can we afford to change them too slowly. We are in a balancing act where knowledge of our users is crucial. But regardless of the rate of change, change must take place, and it must always move us consistently forward in the use of electronic technologies.

Let me share with you one of our most exciting efforts at consumer analysis now underway at Duke. About a year ago, two of our access engineers, Ken Berger and Rich Hines, compiled a document entitled: "The Academic Library of the Future: A Year 2010 Draft Plan for the Duke University Libraries." The document, which was an outline rather than a narrative, described where we will be in the year 2010, where we are now (in relation to where we want to go), and how we will get there. They shared the document widely with library and other university colleagues at Duke.

In describing the library of 2010, Ken and Rich employed a compelling combination of simplicity and boldness. They simply outlined their concept. The first point stated:

Users seldom come into the library building; if they do, it will be for:
- assistance with special problems
- casual/recreational reading (primarily in paper format)
- access to special equipment
- access for those who lack appropriate equipment and/or expertise
- contact with people
- study hall
- functions (e.g., wine and cheese parties)
- instruction—group and individual
  (though some will be done via remote access or off-site visits)

They went on to outline an electronic information environment for which the campus-wide electronic infrastructure (such as fiber optic network) is already largely in place. You will be interested to know that they also projected that library acquisition, personnel and maintenance costs would be sharply lower than today. Other than that, nothing in the document surprised their library colleagues, nor would it surprise you. But what do our users think? Would they be surprised, horrified, or thrilled? That is the real question.

How to answer it was the challenge. Ken, Rich, and I came to believe that if the library asked, that in itself would prejudice the results. It is too similar to dealing with family. So, after consulting with some of our business school faculty and studying the matter, Ken and Rich proposed that the Library retain a marketing agency to find out what our users might think about the changes afoot for libraries and what they might think about alternatives to information as the Library currently makes it available. I agreed, and the process was underway. We eventually took bids and chose a well-respected, regional marketing firm.

By then it was the fall of 1992. The firm we had selected conducted focus groups among the various categories of our users. These groups were video taped and analyzed and were in themselves highly instructive. They convinced me that we were correct in our assessment that our users would say things to an objective third party agency that they would never have said to colleagues. Our marketing agency then proceeded to take the results of the focus group meetings and construct, with the active involvement of Ken and Rich, a survey to be distributed to our students and faculty. That survey was distributed two weeks ago, and the returns are now coming in earnest.

While I am unable to share those larger results with you, let me summarize one of the results of the focus groups. All participants were asked what they thought the characteristics of a good information source were. This is their list:

Accessible
Fast/less time consuming
Labor saving
Free
Computerized
Networked with other libraries
Comprehensive
Expertise available (i.e. librarians)

I share it not only to emphasize that it reflects a movement in the direction of electronic distribution but also to point out that the Duke audience thinks that a good information source includes human help on demand. In pursuing this project, Ken and Rich have taken me up on the challenge of learning more about where our Duke users are in their understanding of the current information environment and of finding out what kind of information environment they would like to see us develop. It is a vital part of access engineering.

CONCLUSION: ACCESS ENGINEERS AND OTHER COLLEAGUES

Reference librarians are not the only librarians who must change, and reference is not the only function now in want of new models for the future. What shall the bibliographer do with fewer books to choose from? And if not with fewer books, then with fewer dollars with which to acquire them? It all amounts to the same outcome. I'm serious about the question. If you become the cartographers, then perhaps bibliographers should become the guides to the Internet and other information/knowledge sources. Maybe you want to reverse the roles. But someone will do it, and bibliographers will, little by little, need new work. And what will the cataloging challenges be in an electronic environment? Surely not what we have thought of as cataloging challenges in our generation.

I make these concluding remarks not because it is your job to redefine everyone's job or create new models for the work of your colleagues. Rather, I do so to make two important points. First, I want just to remind you that you are not here thinking about new reference models while everything else stays the same. No, indeed. The whole library institution is changing, and you are appropriately endeavoring to maintain a place within it for what we have previously known as reference librarians. Second, and this is my last point, I remind you of the change facing your colleagues in order to say that it is alright for you to take some liberties with other departments as you seek to redefine your own. In other words, you cannot develop new models for reference without affecting other aspects of library service. Don't worry about it. Go ahead and do what you have to do. Maybe you'll give them a push in the right direction.

You may be glad to know that my greatest disappointment with the essay on "shaking the foundations" was my inability to find a really suave name. Even I admit that "access engineer" lies somewhere just past awful. It reminds me of a line from another country song about judging things on a scale of one to ten: "Since there ain't no zero, I give you a one." None-the-less, it does symbolize some extraordinarily important aspects of the model I proposed. It emphasizes access, and remember, I mean delivering access; and it emphasizes engineering. In this regard I do not want you to be dependent upon someone else to develop (in the sense of engineer) the delivery systems you design. I bring this up in my conclusion to reemphasize the point that my model moves access engineers into a role that has much more impact on the library as a whole. Determining user needs and developing delivery systems would give you a new central role with, perhaps, an uncomfortable level of responsibility for the design and critique of other library functions.

But then, that is my model. You're here to build a better one. I hope you find it as exciting and invigorating a process as did I, and I look forward to being a part of this Institute. I also wish you the best in this important undertaking, since the continuing intellectual vigor of our institutions depends, in part, on your success.

2 • THE CHANGE PROCESS

Terry Mazany

Consultant
Detroit, Michigan

OVERVIEW

Rethinking reference is the easy part. Doing something with that rethinking is a bit more challenging. The change process for implementing a new and continuously evolving vision of reference requires a shift in our paradigms of change and the leadership for change.

THE PROCESS FOR CHANGE

First, organizational change requires a systems perspective (Figure 1). For effective change we must identify all elements of the system and bring representatives of those elements together.

Comprehensive/Integrative Systems Model for Change

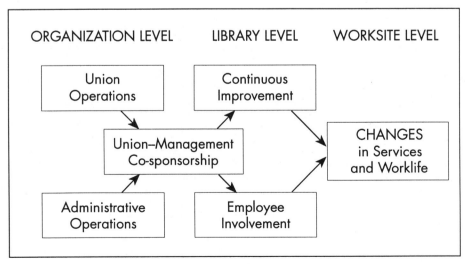

Figure 1

Second, we must adopt a strategic perspective in our planning for change (Figure 2). Unsuccessful change efforts typically begin and end with "how to get there." If we do not know where we are and where we want to be, how to get there will do us little good.

Strategic Planning Model for Change

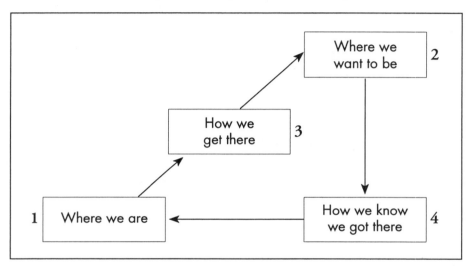

Figure 2

Third, change must be framed as a process of continuous improvement, otherwise we will saddle future generations with the inflexible and out-of-date bureaucracies with which we must currently contend. The process for continuous improvement can be modeled as a developmental process of organizational learning (Figure 3). Typically, organizations proceed through a process of readiness, redesign, and implementation. During this process the members of the organization will progress through attitudinal changes from skepticism to engagement, to excitement as they realize results from their efforts. (Figure 4).

Details of the change process are presented in Figure 5. Key features of this model include a balance of process (the capacity to achieve consensus decisions) with content (the capacity to research and base decisions about innovations on data).

Continuous Improvement Model for Change

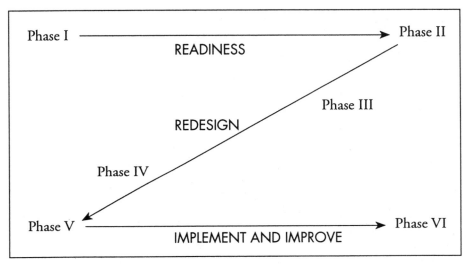

Figure 3

Attitudes About Change

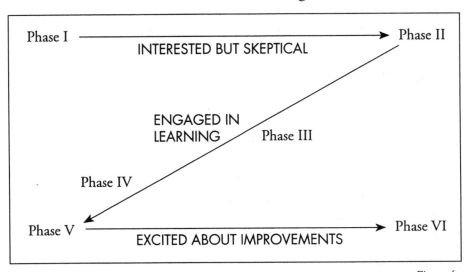

Figure 4

CONTINUOUS IMPROVEMENT MODEL

CHANGE PROCESS	INTERVENTION / SUPPORT

PHASE I: AWARENESS AND TAKING STOCK

• Survey of issues of library change	Overview of current innovations
• Analysis of performance	Research and evaluation support
• Build problem-solving capacity	Problem solving workshop
• Identify short-term action plans	Goal setting workshop
• Construct short-term action plans	Project planning workshop / facilitation

PHASE II: LIBRARY-WIDE AGREEMENTS

• Consensus-building capacity	Consensus building workshop / facilitation
• Structures for involvement	Design principles/facilitation
• Innovative practices	Innovative practices workshop
• Service outcomes	Facilitation
• Essential conditions	Facilitation
• Preliminary vision	Facilitation
• Conflict resolution	Conflict resolution workshop
• Set criteria for improvement model	Facilitation

PHASE III: INQUIRY AND RESEARCH

• Site visits	Site directory
• Literature study	Library/resource room/interactive video/ computer networks
• Study groups	Facilitate
• Data collection	Research and evaluation
• Establish baseline measures	Facilitation
• Innovative strategies	Content workshop
• Experimentation	Design and data collection

PHASE IV: LIBRARY-WIDE CONSENSUS AND COMMITMENT

• Advanced vision	Continuous skill building
• Library redesign project plan	Facilitation
• Authentic Assessment	Facilitation

PHASE V: IMPLEMENTATION

• Identification of success factors	Facilitation
• Project monitoring	Documentation
• Process Assessment	Facilitation

PHASE VI: REFLECTION AND CONTINUOUS IMPROVEMENT

• Evaluation of service outcomes	Assessment
• Project planning	Self-facilitation

FACTORS AFFECTING CHANGE

Substantial research has been conducted concerning the factors affecting the success of change. Perhaps the most comprehensive description of these factors is provided by Fullan (1991). These factors include:

1. NEED AND RELEVANCE OF CHANGE
   - Does the proposed change address a perceived high priority unmet need? To what extent?

2. CLARITY
   - Are the goals of change clearly stated?
   - Is the change clear as to what it means in practice?
   - Is the change presented in an oversimplified manner?

3. COMPLEXITY
   - What extent of change is required of the individuals who must implement it?
   - How difficult are the changes for these individuals?
   - What new skills are required?
   - To what extent does the change require alteration in beliefs, attitudes, and/or behaviors?
   - What new materials will they be required to use?
   - Is the project ambitious enough to make a significant difference?
   - Can the project be divided into manageable components?

4. QUALITY AND PRACTICALITY OF PROGRAMS
   - Are materials necessary for implementation available?
   - Are the materials comprehensive and of sufficient quality?
   - Can the materials be adapted in practice?
   - Do the materials sufficiently cover "how to do it"?

5. THE HISTORY OF INNOVATIVE ATTEMPTS
   - Have the people involved in implementation previously had positive or negative experiences with change?

6. THE ADOPTION PROCESS
   - Is the change being presented in a bureaucratic way?
   - Has the planning process prior to adoption considered both the need the change addresses and the problems of its implementation?
   - Does the plan provide for implementation-level participation?

7. CENTRAL ADMINISTRATION SUPPORT AND INVOLVEMENT
- Does the change have the active support of central administration?
- To what extent are they directly involved in the change effort?

8. STAFF DEVELOPMENT AND PARTICIPATION
- Does the change proposal include a staff development component?
- Who will provide the training and support necessary for implementation?
- To what extent is the training for implementation on going?
- Is it interactive/ Is it cumulative?
- Do the materials allow for participant adaptation to meet the needs of their particular situation?

9. TIME-LINE AND INFORMATION SYSTEMS (FEEDBACK)
- Is sufficient time planned for implementation?
- Is the time line so loose and open ended that progress will be hard to measure?
- Are provisions made for gathering information about the implementation process?
- From what levels will information be gathered?
- What information will be gathered?
- How will it be gathered?
- How will it be used or acted on?

10. BOARD AND COMMUNITY CHARACTERISTICS
- Does the community support the organization?
- Does the community agree with the need for change?
- Does the community support this particular change effort?
- Is the community situation too stable or too turbulent for change to take place?

11. THE ADMINISTRATOR
- Does the project have *active* support of the administrator?
- Does the administrator attend workshops and training sessions?
- Does the administrator interact with staff and understand their concerns?

12. STAFF RELATIONS
- Are the staff working as isolated individuals or do they have an opportunity to interact to learn new meanings, behaviors, and skills?

In addition, the Rand Corporation (Berman and McLaughlin, 1977) conducted a comprehensive study of change and arrived at several generalizations for understanding change:

- Change is a problem of the smallest unit; it is there that the determination is made as to how and whether ideas are implemented.
- Policy cannot mandate change.
- Local variability is the rule; plan for it.
- Initial motivation is not crucial; belief can follow behavior.
- Outside consultants can help, but they must interact with, and adjust effectively, to the local setting.
- Projects narrowly aimed at discrete aspects of the system (problem solving approaches) are likely to fail— bold, comprehensive projects are more likely to produce greater change.
- The content and process of change *both* matter.
- Networking among staff is an effective mechanism for achieving change.
- Removing constraints does not ensure effective practice.
- Project resources do *not* predict outcomes.
- Implementation finally dominates (determines) outcomes.

LEADERSHIP FOR CHANGE

"The best of all leaders is the one who helps people so that, eventually they don't need him." Lao Tzu

A change process reflective of the above description requires leadership consistent with that description. In essence, leadership must be empowering. To understand this type of leadership we must first build a definition of power.

Participatory organizations define power, not as the ability of a person to impose his/her will on others, but as the ability to get things accomplished. Power has two components, authority and influence.

POWER = AUTHORITY + INFLUENCE
(finite)   (infinite)

Authority is the formal power granted to a position such as director or administrator. This power is limited to the number of individuals who hold these power positions. Influence, on the other hand, is exercised by all members of the organization, and those customers, users, or friends of the organization. This power can be conceived of as being infinite. When influence is aligned against authority, influence will prevail. The role of the leader is to align authority with influence.

In traditional organizations, these power tactics are okay:
- Creating dependencies
- Making oneself irreplaceable
- Withholding or providing resources
- Withholding information

In participatory organizations, these tactics don't work. Power is achieved by:
- Openness
- Dependability (trustworthiness)
- Self-development
- Cooperative behavior
- Action orientation

In participatory organizations:
- Leadership is defined as a set of functions which can be shared
- There are many more leadership positions available
- Leaders depend far less on charisma
- The leadership traits which are needed are caring, consideration, and expertise
- Leaders need to be skilled in consensus-building
- Control comes from inside, not from the leader.

The participatory leader:
- Drops or de-emphasizes the coordination and controlling functions
- Becomes a coach/teacher and supporter.

The participatory leader gets results by:
- Building the competence of his/her colleagues
- Making sure that the tools and resources to get the job done are there

- Making sure that people have the economic, physical, psychological, and spiritual incentives to get the job done well
- Managing arrangements between his/her work site and the outside organization and world

The variety of roles for leadership include both maintenance roles (building and/or maintaining team harmony and effectiveness), and task roles (efficiently and effectively accomplishing the task).

MAINTENANCE ROLES:

- **Encourager:** friendly, praises others and their ideas
  "John raises a very good point."

- **Harmonizer:** reconciles disputes and seeks to create openings for consensus
  "I think we can combine both of these ideas and create a better solution."

- **Gatekeeper:** works to ensure that everyone has a chance to be heard
  "I would like to hear from Sarah before we go farther."

- **Standard setter:** expresses standards for the team to use in issue prioritization, brainstorming, and problem solving
  "Remember, we agreed to no criticism during brainstorming."

- **Follower:** good listener who does not speak simply to be heard
  " ? ", or "I have nothing to add that hasn't already been said."

- **Tension reliever:** relieves negative feelings through humor and shifts attention to areas of agreement
  "I know we all love each other, but I can't spend all night with you trying to solve this problem."

TASK ROLES:

- **Initiator:** suggests new ideas or new goals
  "I think we need to explore better ways to network with each other."

- **Information seeker:** asks for relevant facts and information
  "What evidence is there that this method increases access?"

- **Information giver:** provides facts and information, including personal experiences
  "I researched the impact of fibre-optics networks and found there was an increase in speed and performance."

- **Opinion giver:** stating beliefs and opinions as to what should become the team's view
  "I really think that we must involve users on our committees."

- **Clarifier:** restates issues to help the team understand the full meaning
  "If I understand this correctly, we are seeking to recommend to the Dean a new schedule of hours."

- **Elaborator:** builds on previous comments
  "If we take Hal's concern for community service and add to that the idea of database access, I think we can build a plan for an integrated network."

- **Synthesizer:** pulls ideas and suggestions together
  "I think we can combine the ideas counseling programs and neighborhood work projects to help these students."

- **Orienting:** defines and charts the progress of the team
  "We are still talking about college requirements, but remember, we agreed to move on to talk about solutions."

- **Tester:** checks with the team to see if it is ready to reach consensus
  "I am hearing a lot of agreement on this issue. How about if we call for consensus?"

- **Evaluating:** helping the team to evaluate its goals and decisions
  "I think we made a very good decision just now. How do the rest of you feel?"

DYSFUNCTIONAL ROLES:

- **Blocker:** rejects ideas without offering reasons or alternatives
  "That will never work."

- **Aggressor:** criticizes and blames; attacks motives of others
  "This idea would have worked, but they didn't follow through."

- **Attention seeker:** continually focuses the team's attention on him/herself
  "Remember, I was the one who pushed for this solution."

- **Rebel:** refuses to be a team member; sits outside of the group
  "You guys go ahead and do what you want to do. It won't affect me anyway."
- **Recluse:** indifferent and passive; will not voice concerns in the meeting but sabotages agreements afterwards.
  "Fine."
- **Dominator:** asserts authority for the sake of authority; pulls rank and manipulates the team
  "This is not an appropriate issue for this committee. I am the one responsible for this."
- **Magician:** has a hidden agenda which he or she continually introduces into the meeting
  "The only way we can create this schedule is if the reference librarians work only Monday through Friday."

CONSENSUS

A primary means to accomplish the alignment of authority and influence is through the use of consensus decision making. While recognizing that there is a range of decision-making types from command to consensus (Figure 6), issues of planned change are typically well suited to consensus.

Decision-Making Types

Type I:	**Command** *"A decision is made and will be implemented."*
Type II:	**Consultation** *"What are your thoughts on this issue before I have to make a decision?"*
Type III:	**Collaboration** *"I am willing to abide by the consensus of the group if the decision meets these conditions."*
Type IV:	**Consensus** *"We must reach consensus in order to implement this solution."*

Figure 6

25

Consensus can be defined as a systematic process used by a group to make decisions which everyone can support. The dictionary definition is "An opinion held by all or most, general agreement." This contrasts with the definition of compromise which is, "A settlement in which each side makes concessions." This distinction is important. Compromise results in a lose/lose for both parties. For consensus to be effective, both parties must feel that they have achieved a win/win.

Consensus is used for the following purposes:

- Choose among several options
- Insure that everyone has an equal voice
- Promote understanding and ownership
- Allow differences of opinion to surface
- Build unity and common direction
- Encourage mutual benefit thinking
- Prevent sabotage after the decision is made

Groundrules for consensus include:

DO
- Express differences
- Look for common ground
- Listen
- Share information
- Take responsibility for a mutual benefit solution

DON'T
- Vote
- Rush decisions
- Withhold information
- Argue and push positions
- Threaten to withdraw
- Dominate the process
- Compromise

The act of consensus requires a commitment by each member of the group to the decision at hand. This commitment can be gaged individually by applying the following criteria:

- Each participant agrees that he or she has had sufficient opportunity to influence the decision.

- All group members agree to support the decision though it may not be everyone's first choice.

- Everyone is committed to the decision as if it were the first choice of all group members and will support that decision with his/her constituents.

The call for consensus is achieved by placing responsibility on those who feel that these criteria have not been met. The facilitator thus asks:

"Are there any objections?"   Not, *"Is everyone in favor?"*

While it is true that any member of the group may block a decision, that right carries with it certain responsibilities:

- The blocker must explain his/her reasons for blocking to the group

- The blocker must provide another solution or direction to explore

If consensus is not reached, the options include:

- Make no decision
- Table the decision
- Return the decision to the group for additional problem solving
- The committee reaches consensus on an alternative decision-making strategy such as delegating to a decision make
- The committee reaches consensus to vote and let the majority vote decide

Every consensus is the product of a thousand minute consensus building steps. Conditions necessary for consensus to work include:

- Inclusion of all appropriate stakeholders
- Training for all stakeholders
- Foundation agreements
- Creation of a norm of equality
- Identification of mutual goals
- Clear problem definition
- Use of a neutral facilitator for difficult issues
- Openness to all alternatives without judgment
- Establishment of objective criteria to evaluate alternatives
- Rating of the alternatives

Consensus will break down if these conditions are not met. Typical breakdowns include:

- Exclusion of a key stakeholder
- Lack of training for all stakeholders
- No agreement on process
- Domination by one or a few
- Lack of mutual goals
- Disguising solutions as problems
- Criticism of alternatives during brainstorming
- Arbitrary limitations on acceptable alternatives
- Lack of openness to new ideas
- Withholding information
- Hidden agendas
- Impatience and a premature call for consensus
- "Let's vote"
- Threats to withdraw from the process

DESIGNING THE CHANGE PROCESS

The design of a successful process for change is based on a set of design principles:

1. **Self-design:** people support what they create

2. **Inclusion:** all key stakeholders are involved

3. **Representation:** clear accountability and lines of communication to all constituents

4. **Empowerment:** committees are vested with decision-making authority by virtue of participation by the appropriate administrators

5. **Equality:** decisions are made through a consensus process

6. **Integration:** redesign is supported by resource allocation, linkage to budget, and by policies and procedures

In addition, successful change requires the following commitments:

1. **Leadership sponsorship**: the City Manager, University Dean, Department Heads, Union Presidents, and other leaders provide visible leadership, modeling and sponsoring new behaviors and innovative practices

2. **Time**: release time and paid time are provided for all parties to accomplish their training and tasks

3. **Training**: sufficient training is provided to all stakeholders and whole-staff training is provided at the library sites

Consistent with the principle of self-design, the first step in a change process is to conduct a stakeholder analysis and bring all the stakeholders together before any decisions are made. A stakeholder analysis is based on the following questions:

Which organizations will make a difference in the achievement of agreements?

Which individuals will make a difference in the achievement of agreements?

Who will be affected by the agreements?

Who has authority to make decisions? Who has influence to block decisions?

When this or any group first comes together, it must address five main issues in order to develop into an effective committee:

1. **Membership**
   - Who is a member of this group?
   - How did they become a member of this group?
   - Who do they represent?

2. **Goals**
   - What am I trying to accomplish?
   - What is he/she trying to accomplish?
   - What are we trying to accomplish?
   - Do we all agree on the same definitions?

3. **Power**
   - Who has the power in this group?
   - What power does the group have?

4. **Leadership**
- What type of leadership style is needed to best accomplish the task?
- What type of leadership style is needed to best involve others?
- What type of leadership style is needed to best use the resources of the group members?

5. **Operating procedures**
- What rules are needed to make this a good use of our time?
- What rules are needed in order for the group members to feel safe, equal, and free to participate?
- What communication channels do we need to establish to keep our constituents informed and involved?

A role of the facilitator is to be aware of these issues and address them at the beginning of the committee process so that they do not become problems later in the process.

If these issues are not addressed, the committee will become dysfunctional and members will abandon the process. Typically committee breakdowns include:

1. **Membership**
- Changing membership
- Non-participation
- No accountability to constituents
- Failure to include key people

2. **Goals**
- No goals
- Lack of agreement on goals
- Lack of vision of the final product

3. **Power**
- Lack of clarification of authority
- Insufficient authority to accomplish its mission
- Lack of support from persons with authority

4. **Leadership**
- Inability to deal with interpersonal conflicts
- Lack of involvement of all members

5. **Operating procedures**
- Lack of problem-solving skills
- Lack of consensus skills
- No agenda
- Lack of mutual benefit strategies

An effective starting point for newly formed committees is to establish groundrules. Groundrules are designed to secure the following conditions:

- Group members will treat each other with respect
- Different points of view enhance the quality of group discussion and do not lead to alienation of any member
- Each group member feels engaged in the process and a sense of ownership of the solution
- Each group member feels comfortable with, and committed to the decision
- Each group member finds working with the group productive and rewarding

Examples of groundrules include:

- Each person is given the opportunity to speak
- Do not interrupt or talk over another person
- Do not dominate the discussion
- Listen with an open mind
- Make decisions by consensus
- Do not put others down
- Be respectful of each other
- No personal attacks
- Start and end meeting at agreed upon time

CONTINUOUS IMPROVEMENT

Finally, committee effectiveness can be enhanced by applying a set of principles for continuous improvement to the work of the committee. These principles include:

- Placing the customer first
- Being mission driven
- Creating a culture of trust
- Focusing on, and measuring outcomes

- Empowering libraries by pushing control out of the bureaucracy
- Catalyzing stakeholders into action to solve their community's problems
- Creating choices
- Decentralizing authority
- Making decisions based on data
- Preventing problems
- Continuously improving systems

BIBLIOGRAPHY

Berman P. and McLaughlin. *Federal Programs Supporting Educational change: Vol. VII. Factors Affecting Implementation and continuation.*
Santa Monica: Rand Corporation. 1977

Fullan, Michael. *The New Meaning of Educational Change.*
New York: Teachers College Press, 1991.

Gabor, Andrea. *The Man Who Discovered Quality.*
New York: Times Books, 1990

Herrick, Neal Q. *Joint Management and Employee Participation.*
San Francisco: Jossey-Bass, 1991

Senge, Peter M. *The Fifth Discipline.*
New York: Doubleday, 1990

3 • VISION AND VALUES: TOUCHSTONES IN TIMES OF CHANGE

Charles Bunge

Professor, School of Library and Information Studies
University of Wisconsin, Madison

I am happy that I can be involved in this institute and in the larger change process of which I believe it is a part. I hope that, in thinking about and planning changes in reference service, we at this institute— and librarians in general—do not forget the vision and values of reference services that have developed over many years. Indeed, I hope that this vision and these values will be touchstones and guides in the change process. Let me mention a vision of reference service and some of the values that underlie it.

Reference service can be defined as personal assistance given to an individual (or a small sub-group of the library's clientele) whose information need is known (or ascertained) at the time the service is provided. This service adds value to the information resources acquired by the library (and to the cataloging and other processing the resources receive) by helping the individual client find and use the resources successfully.

> "The vision that should guide reference service... is that reference service is a value-added service that is tailored to the unique needs of each individual client."

The vision that should guide reference service, then, is that reference service is a value-added service that is tailored to the unique needs of each individual client. This puts the client and responsive, individualized service to him or her at the center of the value system that guides hour-to-hour, day-to-day reference practice. What are some of the values that are in this value system? We associate values with each side of the reference equation— the client and the librarian.

First the client. We value the dignity of persons and their rights as individuals. Placing value on the dignity of persons means that we are open to the complexity and uniqueness of each client and that we respect his or her own value system. We work cooperatively with the client, seeking to understand and accept his or her information need or request, rather than judging it. We help the client realize his or her own goals, rather than forcing on the client what we think is best. We value freeing and facilitating, rather than controlling and manipulating.

Placing value on the rights of our clients as individuals means that we place a priority on the right to know and on intellectual and academic freedom. A primary value of reference service is equity and equal access to information. The availability of reference service can help library users overcome barriers such as lack of knowledge of resources or ability to find and use them. Because, of all library staff, we have the most direct contact with users, we should be most sensitive and articulate regarding the imperative of equal access to information when, for example, fee structures or restrictions on library and information services are proposed. Other rights of individual clients that we value and protect include the right to privacy and confidentiality in information seeking and use.

Turning to the other side of the reference equation, the reference librarian, what do we value in ourselves and our colleagues? We value professionalism and professional ethics. In our interactions with clients we value competence. We strive to be as knowledgeable and skilled as we can be in providing the service that we purport to offer, and we do not attempt to provide information or advice of a sort or in areas where we are not competent to provide it. We value diligence. We exercise all possible care and effort in responding to queries. We value exercising our judgment independently or objectively, without being influenced by personal philosophies, attitudes, or conflicts of interest. And we value honesty and candor. We should not withhold or manipulate information that would help our client participate in decisions regarding the search for information, its use, and its interpretation.

Finally, what do we value in the institution within which we work? Among many other things, we value the provision of sufficient autonomy and authority to us as professionals to tailor our responses and services to fit the need of each client as an individual. If a reference librarian cannot feel free to make the judgments and take the risks that are involved in client-centered reference service, it will be very hard for him or her to hold the vision or act on the values that I have sketched out above.

Let me close with a quote from Francois Jacob (The Possible and the Actual, Pantheon, 1982) that I came upon in an article by Willie Parson (*College and Research Libraries*, September 1984). "Whether in a social group or in an individual, human life always involves a continuous dialogue between the possible and the actual. A subtle mixture of belief, knowledge, and imagination builds before us an ever-changing picture of the possible. It is on this image that we mold our desire and fears. It is to this possible that we adjust our behavior and actions." We reference librarians place the highest value on helping our clients develop their sense of the actual and conception of the possible. As we plan and implement changes in our reference services, I hope that this conference helps each of us, by ourselves and in our libraries, participate in that dialogue between the actual and the potential.

4 • ALLIES, PARTNERS AND COMPETITORS

Suzanne Calpestri

Head, Library Cooperative Services
University of California, Berkeley

Tomorrow I will host a discussion group in which participants can explore ideas about the role of allies, partners, and competitors in the new reference setting. My remarks this morning are designed to start you thinking about this topic.

As we re-examine library reference service and develop new models of service we will need to look outward and involve others beyond the reference department, the library, the campus and the community. We will find the means to support new service models by restructuring relationships with current associates and by cultivating partnerships with heretofore non-traditional partners, including those we have viewed as competitors and rivals. These newly formed partnerships will be important not only in shaping new service models for reference but will also be the means by which reference departments can acquire expanded and future-oriented resources necessary for reference librarians to be full participants in the creation and distribution of information within the scholarly community.

NEW PRESSURES

The pressures on reference departments today are intense. Information—our primary commodity—is being generated at ever-increasing rates and is becoming available in a variety of expensive formats that challenge even the healthiest financial allotments of the past. Today, of course, no one has those generous budgets. Instead, we are working with severely reduced allocations that are woefully inadequate to meet the information explosion, price inflation for that information, and the devaluation of the American dollar when dealing in the international market. Simultaneously, users' needs for information and expectations for service are at an all-time high. Patrons expect us to provide all the same services we have in the past along with an array of new services connected with new technologies requiring additional expertise on our part. These demands would challenge even the most robust and hearty staff, but the workforce at most libraries has been seriously reduced in overall numbers and experience. Those library workers who are left are exhausted from overload caused by attrition and layoffs. Nonetheless, we are still trying to do it all.

OLD SOLUTIONS

For the most part, reference work in our libraries is driven by individualism, self-reliance, and do-it-yourself thinking. Working from this general outlook, we have tried to increase our personal capacity through automation and mechanization. We have multi-plexed our systems and multi-plexed ourselves. With voice mail we can answer the phone and handle in-person questions simultaneously. It is so easy to believe we can do it all by going just a little bit faster. We have tried reorganization in an effort to address these pressures, but in most cases this has been more like shifting the pressure than relieving or eliminating it. For example, to save staff, some departments have eliminated regular group catalog instruction only to find themselves overburdened at the information desk with endless routine questions that had been handled in the catalog instruction course. For the most part, reorganization within the reference department has not released staff to provide new or different services.

Within the library, our severely limited budgets and departmental allocation process set departments up to compete with each other, and the successful department head is the one most skilled in cut-throat competition aimed at wiping out other departments that would vie for the precious resources available. We have budget hearings to argue the merits of the catalog department's need for money to do retrospective conversion versus the reference department's need to staff the desk and provide instructional service, or the mail division's need to stay within budget by using the cheapest delivery system versus the ILL department's need to get the package to its destination at any cost. Success is measured in terms of who gets the biggest budget increase. When Technical Services does not get funding to hire a specialist to catalog African literature in tribal languages because the money went to Public Services needing to keep all information desks staffed, the reference staff spends hours searching the shelves to answer a patron question requiring that African material. And sometimes the question goes unanswered with a quick comment like, "That material is not available yet." Perhaps as a last resort we will suggest another inadequate option—Interlibrary Loan—a transaction in which the library will spend $30.00 to borrow what we own but have not catalogued, and therefore cannot make available. The patron will spend three weeks waiting for the information needed today, contained in a book sitting in a room just steps away. There are lots of losses in this strategy.

When competition does not seem appropriate we compromise. Under the best circumstances we win something and, if we're lucky, we lose only a little. Rather than respond to patron demands for longer service hours, we compromise and yield to the few who want to have a library in their office building. We keep all branch libraries open, but for only a few hours, and we trust that the patrons will understand the severity of our budget situation and forgive us for any inconvenience we cause them.

In other instances, we have tried to ration our resources by adopting exclusionary practices and becoming insular. We have re-organized service delivery, often causing increased patron inconvenience, and we have quietly hoped this will cause some to give up altogether, thus keeping the demand for service at a level we can at least manage. Sometimes we take the phone off the hook or eliminate telephone service altogether. But this gets no one off the hook. We know full well that many of our patrons find it essential to use the library from their home or office. Increasingly, reference service is becoming available only to those who will go to the greatest trouble to use the library. And their numbers are all we can handle.

UNACCEPTABLE RESULTS

These strategies so far have hampered the patron's ability to use the library's collections and services and thus reduced the demand for our offerings. Sadly, these strategies have not led to increased resources for the library, nor have they done much to protect what we had. We certainly do not have increased funding support; we have less. The staff is demoralized. People work harder than ever and fall farther behind. Excellence in service is rare—an exception to the rule. Service is usually mediocre, and all too often it is completely inadequate or unavailable. Most disturbing of all, patrons' support for the library is eroding. They are disgruntled when they find it impossible to get very basic information that is reliable. They ask, "Is the library going to be open on Sundays this month?" The brochure says one thing, the online catalog says something else, and the message on the phone machine agrees with neither; and there is no one to ask in person. In a situation like this, some patrons will complain, others will quietly leave. They all will look elsewhere for another service to fill their needs if we fail them.

NEW OUTCOMES

In this symposium we are challenging ourselves to develop models of reference service that will have different outcomes. We want our work as reference librarians to remain a vital and necessary element in the information chain supporting academic research. This will require new skills and different thinking than has been part of the reference departments until now. Looking outward to others will not be easy; we have little experience in doing so. We may also not be comfortable engaging others for help because it will mean relinquishing some control. But we must. We do not have the capacity to succeed in isolation. The world is increasingly interdependent, and we need to follow that trend.

A NEW WAY OF DOING BUSINESS

It is our job to identify the unique role of reference librarians in the scholar's work. We reference librarians from universities and colleges across the country must determine the distinctive skills and expertise that we contribute to the production of scholarly information. What business are we in? Are we in the teaching business, the information-delivery business, the information-creation business or the archiving business? Or is it something else? Our visions and values shared in discussions may inform our responses to these queries. By answering these questions we will know where to focus our efforts and our talents, rather than trying to do it all. With this knowledge, we can better identify those people and groups that will be needed to promote scholarly information, of which we are a part. Within the library, it may be the catalog department, the systems office, or the mail service. If we have relied on these departments in the past, will we rely on them in the future? And if so, how will our relationship with them need to change? Are these departments rethinking their services and if so how are we involved in those discussions? And how are we involving them in our discussions about new reference models? Are we collaborating in the development of our new models or are we working in our old familiar patterns in which one department develops a plan which is then reviewed by others? Are we developing realistic positions regarding finite resources and negotiating compromises to develop cooperative agreements, or are we identifying our interests and issues as reference staff so that we can join with others to expand the resources necessary to provide excellence in reference service within the university library?

Beyond the libraries we will find other allies, and we will need to ask the same questions of these potential partners. In what way might the faculty, research units, the computer center, the student learning center, the bookstore and others become our partners? Will we involve these players in developing our models? And if so, how? Will we vie with the computer center for a reporting line or will we join forces to develop services that take advantage of each of our unique resources in support of the scholarly enterprise? How can we develop relations with publishers, database producers and other businesses, all of whom we have traditionally viewed as rivals? Still others might be involved. Copy services may have something else to offer with their experience in print-on-demand course readers that in some measure have replaced the reserve-book function that libraries used to offer exclusively. What can we learn from them about document delivery on demand and customized information? And how will we ensure the success of the patron when success depends on so many elements outside our sphere of direct control?

Our success will depend on our ability to bring together a new cast of characters to provide the service patrons need and our skill in learning to collaborate in our work. Instead of designing minimal services driven by budget and staffing shortages, we will design services based on the highest level that patrons require and we will support these by new alliances that bring together the resources required for those services to thrive. If we can collaborate and co-ordinate successfully, we will achieve excellence in service and it will be consistent and sustainable—failure will be the exception. We will seek out resources and partnerships that provide opportunities to further the value of the library for scholarly work—we will not wait for opportunities to come to us. And we will be visible. Rather than hope that patrons don't notice when we cut an hour of service, we will make every service hour count. Patrons will know what we do in reference and how we are related to their work.

We are rethinking reference because the pressures in our environment threatens us with obsolescence. Our work in this symposium is not an academic drill but an exercise necessary for the survival of the academic library. It is a big job and the stakes are high. The models we develop in this symposium and those we develop in our libraries need to include unfamiliar partners and strategic relationships.

5 • RETHINKING THE REFERENCE DESK

Virginia Massey-Burzio

Head of Resource Services, Milton S. Eisenhower Library
Johns Hopkins University, Baltimore, Maryland

First I will briefly describe the research consultation model as it was set up at Brandeis in March 1990 and at Hopkins in Oct. 1992. Both are research institutions similar in size. Brandeis has about 3000 students and Hopkins about 6000. Hopkins, however, has a large school of Continuing Studies with about 14,000 students. I will then discuss some practical and conceptual issues raised by this model.

DESCRIPTION

In essence an Information Desk and a Research Consultation Service replace the traditional reference desk in this model. The purpose of the information desk is to provide directional and brief informational assistance that takes no longer than a few minutes to convey. It is also to screen questions and make proper referrals to librarians. When I was at Brandeis, the Information Desk was staffed by graduate students. At Hopkins the Information Desk is staffed by support staff and graduate students. Both Brandeis and Hopkins use student monitors to man their electronic information services.

The Research Consultation Office is staffed by librarians who provide answers to longer, more complex questions, as well as assist new users with an introduction to the library and/or scholars with research assistance in their own area or a new area. The office—an enclosed, private space with large windows—is designed to provide the optimal environment to enhance the client-professional interaction. The numerous directional and brief informational questions, as well as the constantly ringing phone, associated with the traditional reference desk, do not interrupt transactions with clients. Patrons respect the privacy of the consultation. The enclosed office design of the consultation office, in other words, sends a clear message to the patron that a private professional consultation is in progress. The research

> The traditional reference desk looks like a service that does not expect to be taken seriously.

consultation office at both institutions is adjacent to the Information Desk, although the one at Hopkins is out of sight of the Information Desk. The librarians at Hopkins are subject specialists, consequently the librarian in the Research Consultation Office may refer a patron further on to a more appropriate subject specialist. The decision was made to have the research consultation librarian make this referral rather than Information Desk staff, although the issue will be revisited at a later date. The Hopkins librarians are assigned to two to five departments each, with a responsibility to make themselves known and to know their faculty and students, and to exert a presence in their academic departments. In light of this emphasis, eventually eliminating even the research consultation office will be considered at a later date. In other words, we are not wedded to a single professional service space in the library. Already one librarian has office hours in her academic department and another has been asked by one of her departments to come and have office hours. We envision patrons going directly to the office of the appropriate librarian either in the library or in the academic department, perhaps with a system of office hours, appointments and drop-ins.

An evaluation is in progress now at Brandeis. One is planned at Hopkins in the fall of this year. It is already clear, however, that the model is a success in that it improves the quality of the interaction between the patron and the librarian to the benefit of both.

PRACTICAL ISSUES

This research consultation model addresses both practical and conceptual issues surrounding information service delivery.

The most practical issue, of course, is the overwhelming patron demand brought on mostly by the new electronic information technologies. This demand has challenged our most cherished service beliefs. Reference librarians can wax rather eloquently and at length about the importance of being available, establishing eye contact, being warm, friendly and open, and answering even the most basic question with enthusiasm in order to establish a relationship of trust with the patron, et cetera et cetera. However, being warm and friendly with long lines at a reference desk while trying to man a constantly ringing phone and fielding questions about a paper jam is stressing out even the most saintly of reference librarians. Perhaps even more critical are the studies that have been done since the 1970's that indicate that reference service is nowhere near as successful as we had thought it was. Instead of challenging these studies, as some have done, or ignoring them, as most of us have, we should be questioning our service model. Why do we pattern it after the department store sales clerk model—hardly an intellectual transaction—instead of, for example, the lawyer-client model, a much more similar transaction? The traditional reference desk looks like a service that does not expect to be taken seriously. Social scientists have noted this phenomena. As one said, "...unlike other professionals the librarian must establish the professional relationship with the other person under a severe restriction of time while also being limited to a chance condition of meeting in public. The fact that professional library service succeeds at all is amazing."[1]

The failure of the traditional reference desk in my view suggests that we have overstressed user accessibility to the librarian to the detriment of user needs and the most judicious use of professional librarians. User accessibility to the librarian is almost a sacred cow as strongly advocated by 20-year veterans as new library school graduates. Yet there is no convincing evidence in existence to suggest why this should be such an overriding service value.

The research consultation model shares the burden of patron demand with non-librarians and better utilizes the skills of each. When reference librarians are answering so many high-volume, but low-level questions, they cannot spend too much time with any one patron, no matter how complicated or difficult the patron's question may be. Ironically, the very patron who needs help with the type of question that librarians are most exclusively equipped to answer, is the one who loses in the traditional reference model. Not only is the patron not being well served, but the professional expertise of the librarian is not being utilized. It is more cost effective to utilize students or other non-professional personnel to handle low-level, orientation-type questions. Beth S. Woodard argues that students, if well trained, are best able to handle these types of questions.[2] Miller and Rettig have pointed out quite rightly that libraries are squandering their professional personnel on answering simple directional questions or whether or not the library owns a specific item.[3]

CONCEPTUAL ISSUES

Conceptually, the model begins to address the role of the academic reference librarian and creates both a new image for the librarian and a new relationship between the librarian and the patron. It is clear that it is the latter that resonates with academic librarians. Feedback on the consultation service indicates that receiving expert help increases the value that patrons place on the reference librarian's work. Many patrons have also pointed out the value of having the undivided attention of a librarian. An indication of this and one of the biggest surprises has been how verbal patrons have become in expressing their needs. Clearly, the more verbal they are, the more we are able to help them get what they need.

Joan Durrance did a study which indicates that the traditional reference desk makes it difficult for library users to establish a relationship with someone in the library, to be able to return to someone that they had built up a relationship with to get additional help because they are unsure whether they have talked to a librarian, a library assistant or a student.[4] And, to take it further, whether to reveal to that person what the library user feels may be his or her ignorance. Library users also must wonder whether the person behind the desk or counter has the capability or expertise to understand their research problems. Durrance points out that people do not get confused about whether they are talking to a doctor or a nurse, a lawyer or a legal secretary, a loan officer or a bank teller. The library professional seems to be alone in having this problem. In fact, in most professions the client-professional interaction is controlled by the professional with the result that the interaction is enhanced.

In the Research Consultation Office it is very clear to patrons that they are talking to a professional. The privacy of the consultation may also be a factor in improving the interaction. Jo Bell Whitlatch has pointed out that the "overall effects of giving and receiving service in an environment where librarians are in constant demand and where demand is also unpredictable may condition both librarians and users to provide and expect extremely short interaction times."[5] This alternative setting obviously overcomes this problem and improves the quality of the interaction.

But, interestingly enough, it is not the role of the librarian that people want to discuss or argue about, an issue that is, in my view, in dire need of being discussed. Rather the focus of their questions and concerns lie almost solely with the role of the staff at the Information Desk. I have wondered if it is because this segment of the model is, in fact, weak – that is, we can't really train non-librarians to properly interview, answer or refer questions, as some librarians claim. Or is it because it represents a threat to what we thought was our role? Are we reluctant to give up the familiar because we fear the unknown? For those of you familiar with the Strategic Visions Steering Committee, just consider the list of qualities they have enumerated as being needed by the future librarian. In fact, the list was devised from current job ads. The future is now. Among public service managers in the halls and corridors of conferences, the subject of discussion is the problems we are having moving librarians from traditional roles to new ones. Many of us have been surprised at the reluctance of some librarians to do what we consider more interesting work. Many questions asked at an Information Desk or a traditional reference desk are, if you will pardon my saying the unthinkable, just plain boring and repetitive. Bill Miller said it less baldly and perhaps more elegantly: "I for one was always glad to be working with the student assistants; they gave me the chance to indulge in the unaccustomed luxury of doing some real reference work."[6]

Larry Oberg has pointed out in his article, "The Emergence of the Paraprofessional in Academic Libraries,"[7] that the difference in roles between librarians and paraprofessionals has blurred because librarians seem reluctant to give up aspects of their work which no longer need to be performed by them. This not only confuses paraprofessionals, who then want the same money and prestige, but also confuses our clientele, who perceive librarians and paraprofessionals to be doing the same thing. He points out that this perception erodes the quality of contacts between the library and its clientele and that librarians need to communicate a clearer image of who they are and what they do. I couldn't agree more. Instead of going around in circles on the Information Desk, we need to recast the issue by looking at ourselves and what we are especially qualified and trained to do, looking at our users and what they really need and then looking at the Information Desk and its role.

CONCLUSION

My discussion of this model is not necessarily to persuade you to replicate this model in your library, but to take note of the advantages of this change in the reference environment and to consider where to go from here, building on this experience. I suspect the possibilities exhibited here are only the tip of the iceberg.

Nina Matheson, retiring director of the Johns Hopkins Medical Library, which she so successfully fashioned into a lively, innovative enterprise that creates information with its clientele, warns us that thinking that libraries are in an evolutionary process rather than a revolutionary one is a dangerously passive perspective. She advises us—and I take her very seriously because of her success—to systematically abandon assumptions and mind-sets, think the unthinkable, and ask ourselves hard questions. Upon setting out on our voyage of discovery in order to find new lands, we realize that we must, by necessity, lose sight of the shore.[8]

REFERENCES

1. Thomas Lee Eichman, "Speech Action in the Library," in *Linguistics and the Professions*, edited by Robert DiPietro (Norwood, N.J. Ablex, 1982), p. 256.

2. Beth S. Woodard, "Effectiveness of an Information Desk Staffed by Graduate Students and Nonprofessionals, " *College & Research Libraries* 50 (July 1989) : 455-467.

3. Constance Miller and James Rettig, "Reference Obsolescence," *Reference Quarterly* 25 (Fall 1985) : 57.

4. Joan Durrance, "Reference Success: Does the 55 Percent Rule Tell the Whole Story?" *Library Journal* 114 (April 15, 1989): 31-36.

5. Jo Bell Whitlatch, The Role of the Academic Reference Librarian (New York: Greenwood Press, 1990), 8.

6. William Miller, "Breaking the Pattern of Reference Work Burnout," *Journal of Academic Librarianship* 18 (November 1992): 281.

7. Larry R. Oberg, "The Emergence of the Paraprofessional in Academic Libraries: Perceptions and Realities", *College & Research Libraries* 53 (March 1992) : 100-101.

8. Nina Matheson, "The Academic Library Nexus", *College & Research Libraries* 45 (May 1984) : 208

6 • MAKING TOUGH CHOICES: THE PAIN, THE REWARDS, AND THE REALITY AT VIRGINIA TECH

Frances O. Painter

Director of Administrative Services
Virginia Tech University Libraries, Blacksburg

I received my Masters of Library Science degree in the spring of 1973 in an outdoor graduation ceremony on the campus of George Peabody College in Nashville, Tennessee. I had a job—I had been hired as a cataloger in the library of the University of Tennessee, a position which came with the faculty rank of Instructor and the salary of $9000 a year. This was in the days immediately preceding OCLC, and in the Cataloging Department, we typed and photoduplicated sets of catalog cards and carefully filed them into the public catalog and the shelf list. My colleagues in Public Services and Collection Development were striving to develop a rich, comprehensive collection, and to assist students in deciphering how we had organized and housed the books and journals. One of my best friends came into my office a few weeks ago, gazed out the window, and said, "you know, this library and my work in it are nothing like what I thought I'd be doing as a librarian. I'm not sure what I bring to work these days ... It was never like this before." My friend is overpowered sometimes—indeed we all are—by the new images, new metaphors, new ways of thinking about our library organization. Today, powerful forces are prompting us into new services, roles, and relationships.

Underlying our organizational change is an undeniable chill in the financial air in Virginia and a shift in the state's perception of higher education. Virginia Tech has lost $38 million university wide in operating reductions and salary losses. More than 300 positions were abolished—13 of them from the University Libraries. Salaries were frozen from July 1990 thru December 1992. Tuition and fee increases have replaced about $10 million, leaving the University with a net annual loss of $27 million. State councils and commissions are stridently calling for a re-structuring of higher education. Their posture is unmistakably critical. Virginia legisla-

> There has always been some difference between the University's financial circumstances and its aspirations, but that difference is growing into a wide gap.

tors and taxpayers are no longer willing to afford the colleges and universities they have established. There has always been some difference between the University's financial circumstances and its aspirations, but that difference is growing into a wide gap. There has been a dramatic shift of costs from the state to individual students and parents. We now rank 9th in tuition among all land grant universities. Certainly we must seek sources of revenue outside state appropriations, but competition for these funds is keen. It will not be possible to recapture our expectations with increasing tuition and outside sources. As our Provost, Fred Carlisle, has stated, "Virginia Tech must look to basic internal change to make up that difference. We are learning that we must select, choose, and sharpen our priorities. We should start thinking about change through substitution and not through addition. This has been the talk for years, but the necessity of acting on these words is very real." Of course, the University Libraries are swept along by this stream. These changes have become a part of our daily working lives—altering our organization, revising our outlook, changing our organizational character, and transforming us all in the process. We now, more than ever, must convince the University that we really do work hard and are effective and efficient. We have to get the most out of, not just get by with our portion of the University's budget.

EMPHASIS ON SERVICE

Technology is clearly changing conditions of work in libraries. We've all observed and experienced them in our own workplace. We are moving away from the concept of a library as a building, or a place. Our campus outreach effort this spring was entitled "You don't have to come to the library to ..." and listed eight services available to anyone with a user-id to access the campus mainframe computer. Our emphasis is shifting to access, and to the delivery of information. Our organizational character and culture are changing too, raising new issues for library management. At Virginia Tech, we have re-examined our mission, adjusted our organizational structure, and come to consensus on goals and objectives, and developed yearly action plans. The new constrained educational economy in Virginia provides a legitimate and pressing importance to our examination of our programs and services—we have to find out what to add, what to sustain, and what to limit, consolidate, or discontinue. Our vision of service is our sense of direction. As we study and re-evaluate the role of the library in the University, we can not help but re-evaluate the appropriate distribution of resources within the library. There is an old business school joke about a company trying to present its decline in the best possible terms for the annual report. A review of the year's work begins with the statement, "Having lost sight of our objectives, we re-doubled our efforts." This same concept is parodied in today's human resource management literature as "Empower the Aimless!" Prior to 1991, many of our managers and employees had neither a clear view of their own departments' objectives, nor an understanding of the role that they could play in our overall strategic plan. I can say with confidence now that most of our librarians, support staff, and student workers can express what their department and even their individual job duties contribute to patron satisfaction. We began with a mission and goals statement, to articulate for everyone our reason for being. Ours has three parts—Service, Collections, and Organizational Climate, and each part reflects back onto our customer service emphasis. Let me read you just three examples of library-wide goals:

* Review internal library procedures with better user service as a primary consideration.
* Develop administrative systems that facilitate the productivity of our staff and our users.
* Monitor and evaluate the requirements of users and reallocate available resources accordingly.

Each year we prepare a library-wide goals and objectives document and go one step further into action plans—definable or measurable steps we will take during the year in support of our objectives. A look at this document precedes any budget planning sessions and decisions—that includes our materials budget, our personnel budget, and our operating budget. Each department also prepares its own annual goals and objectives and action plans, emphasizing its key objectives and major action steps. We have established a planning calendar and a schedule to monitor our progress, make adjustments, and report results. Our budget process is much more open. Our staff do take this involvement seriously, and some of our more innovative plans and more draconian cost-cutting measures have come from staff at levels below traditional "management" levels. They have good ideas for a better way to do their own jobs.

A second service (and survival) strategy is to determine users' needs. We need to know what we can do to help our users gain access to information more effectively. We conduct a regular user survey in the spring—the survey is mailed to faculty members, and we sample patrons coming into the building. One year, this survey indicated that the biggest source of frustration among our library users was our photocopy operation. We were able to re-structure the unit and obtain new, higher-capacity machines based upon these expressed needs—not going on our own guesses. This year's survey indicates a real problem in our bibliographic instruction. Our patrons are unaware of the finer points and some of the most powerful aspects of our online catalog. We believe that it is so easy to get some results from a search that our patrons often stop their search and don't go on beyond the basics. They reported dissatisfaction with our system and made suggestions to improve it that for the most part already exist. We only brought up Boolean searching and keyword searching last year, and we seem to have reached the heavy library users successfully, but not so much the less devoted user, or the user not as familiar with our system. We have our work cut out for us, and we used these comments to make a decision to recruit for two more reference instructional librarians. With the discussion based upon this expressed need, and our stated goals and objectives, there is much more support of this employment, and much less of the territorial sniping and unproductive competition for a vacant faculty position that we experienced in the past.

We also continually look for more personal ways to involve our library patrons in the planning and development of our services. We have successfully campaigned to ensure that librarians and library staff participate fully in University governance through membership on the Faculty Senate, the Staff Senate, and operational committees. We use the University Library Committee as a sounding board—At this committee's request, we somewhat reluctantly undertook to measure periodicals use within our main library. The experience was an excellent first step for our staff in library-wide involvement in methodology and measurement, and of course the data gathered proved useful in our later $300,000 serials cut (1250 titles). Administering this serials cancellation project taught us another useful lesson in determining our users' needs. We did take a risk in involving departmental faculty as we did. We were completely open about our plans and our budget. We did give out more information about what goes on in our materials budget. We came to grips with the fact of University life that our materials budget is not a document we could keep secret forever. As my colleague Paul Metz puts it, "It's better to share information if asked than to surrender it after being ordered to." Did we lose some control? Maybe. But did we find out what journals our faculty need to do their job effectively? Yes. Other user survey techniques we've implemented include involving students and faculty in the evaluation of CD-Rom products for purchase, and asking people coming into the building to identify their function within the University and their purpose for visiting the library (based upon this survey, we developed a bibliographic instruction course aimed at departmental secretaries and administrative assistants).

TRAINING

It's one thing to set goals and survey users. The real impact of service emphasis in a library is the changes it brings about in conditions of work—changes observed and experienced in our jobs. Let's look at some of these. First and foremost, our library staff require training. Even with all the ways that electronic information sources can help our users, our service will be effective only if our staff knows how to use them. It's easy to skim the top of all our technology. Most of our faculty and student users are more technically sophisticated than ever before, but they still need us to explain how to use the systems we have. Our interpersonal skills are often as important as our technological savvy.

At Virginia Tech, our old organizational structure encouraged the development of pockets of expertise. Each reference department had its own philosophy about, and its own way of working with library users. We did not have a unified force that consistently connected with our patrons. We now have two reference departments instead of four, and we emphasize that we are here for the customer—we don't always do what they want, but we listen thoughtfully to their complaints and questions and consider all the possibilities. We try to listen, analyze, and empathize before we make judgments. We tend to do a lot of hiring at the beginning professional level—individuals with less than four years of post-MLS experience. It is more important now than ever that our librarians work well with others, whatever their position in the library, and we look for this as much as subject expertise when we interview. We need people who can wear more than one hat at work; with a thinner staff, we need people who can accept broader responsibilities and tolerate ambiguity.

I don't see much in the human resources literature now about what we used to call job enrichment, and I think it's been replaced by coping with choices and stress. We are battered every day with more choices and changes. We have a static budget, and an ever-increasing menu of new electronic products and services. Our customers' expectations are rising too. We have to stretch our materials budgets, and we have to finance the required hardware and software and think about obsolescence. But, if we expect good front-line service, we must pay attention to teaching our staff to be able to deal with stress. We have to learn to "manage change," or, more accurately for most of us, we have to learn to manage our lives at work in an environment of constant change. Even with increased pressure on our operating budget, we maintain and protect a level of travel and development funding for librarians and staff. We have a policy on job rotation for librarians and staff to gain knowledge and understanding of other departments' operations. Our reference departments and our access services departments have been meeting together several times a year to explore their mutual concerns. We recognize the need to carve out time for our reference librarians to study, evaluate, and learn new products, and we support this with temporary staff assistance. We are moving away from a reliance on salary savings to balance the operating budget, and are filling vacancies promptly. We were successful in receiving funding for graduate assistants to staff the reference desk, and we continue to seek outside support for travel and development. Our online catalog vendor made a travel fund for library staff available this year. Again, with our goals and objectives we can make these decisions to contribute to improved patron service.

REVISING JOBS, SPREADING RESPONSIBILITIES

> We are still working on letting go of the old, relinquishing some of our most cherished ideas, giving up some of our assumptions about what works.

Looking at our organizational structure made us seek simpler ways to lead the Libraries, ones that require less administrative effort and produce less stress than our old practices. We eliminated the Assistant Director level; department heads now report directly to the University Librarian. We re-thought our "usual and customary" committee and meeting structure. We created new formal and informal communication channels. This has not always been comfortable, but I'm coming to believe strongly that the deep reality of our organizational life is constant flux and unpredictability. I don't believe anymore that one morning everything will settle down, and be crystal clear to me. Now I see my challenge as accepting volatility, instability, vulnerability, risk, and uncertainty. My response, and everyone in the library's personal reaction, has to be flexibility, creativity, and entrepreneurship. Certainly, we've only begun to discover and create the new organizational forms that will exist in years to come. We are still working on letting go of the old, relinquishing some of our most cherished ideas, giving up some of our assumptions about what works. Einstein told us that no problem can be solved from the same consciousness that created it; we have to learn to see the world anew. Let me tell you some of the new images of organization we're trying to work with.

One of the most disturbing changes for me, and for many of my colleagues, was relinquishing control. Our budget decisions are made in a much larger group now, and those decisions are communicated as they never were before. There is continuous review and examination of our budget allocations in light of our stated goals and objectives. Department heads have more approval authority, and more accountability. We've gone to great lengths to dispel the air of secrecy about our budget. We taught all our employees about salary savings, telecommunications costs, materials budget formulas, auxiliary operations, and cost recoveries. The more people understand, the more they want to see the results. They want to know how well we're doing, and understand what their contribution is.

I've finally been successful this spring in convincing the University's Personnel Services Department to assist us in a library-wide review of the classifications assigned to our library support staff. Our existing classification descriptions had long been left in the dust by the changes in library work over the years. We also needed to revise our previous narrowly specific job descriptions to be able to move scarce personnel resources to where they're needed. We have prepared a written report of the components of staff job satisfaction in the libraries—what makes our staff feel good about working here. We found that what our staff enjoy most is recognition of their achievements, more responsibility, the chance for new assignments and advancement, and the opportunities for growth in knowledge. We just received the report of the Task Force on Recognition of Achievement, and we will be implementing a year-round program

55

of varied recognitions. We are working with the University to provide more flexibility in work schedules, including four-day work weeks and nine-month appointments for staff and faculty. We continue to emphasize our liberal approval of tuition waivers, job rotation within the libraries, and generous travel and development funding.

Our Humanities/Social Sciences Reference Department had expressed interest in a limited-term departmental chair instead of a department head, and when the position became vacant, we implemented such a policy. Each tenured faculty member of the department is eligible for election to a term of three to five years as department chair; the chair is expected to express collegial leadership rather than traditional management and hierarchial organization. So far, this has been a successful experiment. We're seeing more effective communication and increased internal participation and collective responsibility for departmental decisions.

We go out of our way to keep track of our various committees and task forces, with a regular reporting system in our monthly Library Forum meetings and in our online weekly news bulletin. A lot of what we're doing is anticipating credibility problems before they arise. I don't think people passively accept leadership anymore—they want to evaluate the situation for themselves. Like most large organizations, we have a history of defensive behavior and people who felt a need to control information. It takes a long time to build feelings of trust, and to feel comfortable with moving out of the familiar and safe. It will take us some time to develop the tolerance for gaps in information that inevitably occur in a fast-moving organization. We've been criticized at times for the delay in decision making that deeper communication efforts require, and some individuals feel overburdened with all this additional information. But the majority believe they are more effective because they are better informed.

I could not stand here and tell you that we have no library employees who refuse to change their habits, refuse to yield decision-making control, or refuse to listen to anyone who suggests a different way—sure we do. I've come to see that most of these people feel that they've been betrayed, that they aren't doing what they were originally hired to do. Or they feel that they are underskilled, and are embarrassed by their lack of competence or knowledge. Or they feel they can coast and let their colleagues carry the weight. We do spend time identifying these people, counseling them, re-educating them. We have a contract with a local psychological counseling firm to provide conflict resolution and mediation services. We are a very inter-dependent organization and we need to be aware of the impact our communications and relationships have to either help or hinder our library colleagues as they do their jobs, and how important this contribution is to the success of the entire library.

CHANGE IS THE STATUS QUO

In conclusion, I do realize that most of our projects and programs could come about in a library without a mandate for change, but I'm not sure they would be as transforming, and I'm not sure we would be so conscious of the need to use our brains, and to give oddball ideas a fair and careful hearing. We no longer have the comfort of gravitating to our old wisdom and our old successes. As a personnel officer, one of the most telling employment references I ever heard was the time I asked a reference about a candidate's listening skills and was told, "Since he already knows everything, he has never been confused by a new thought." I hope you and I never get that far. We have to reinvent the interactions of our organizational goals, people, processes, and technology, and accept change as the new status quo at every employee's level.

7 • FROM VISION TO REALITY: CHANGE AT THE UNIVERSITY OF IOWA

Janice Simmons-Welburn

Head of Reference, Main Library
University of Iowa Libraries, Iowa City

I have been asked to speak about change and the provision of reference and information services in academic libraries, with specific regard to what we are engaged in at the University of Iowa. I intend to discuss, in a nutshell, the old and new realities for reference and information services, and the link between them—that of creating a vision and planning strategically toward that vision.

It is imperative at the outset that I establish a context in which we can understand how reference and information services are structured at our university. We are designing new approaches to Information Services that are mindful of two important considerations: First, the university is a decentralized, loosely coupled organization. Second, systemwide reference services are loosely coupled as well. Karl Weick's theory of loose coupling suggests that the elements of our system of reference service are—like the structure of the university and its academic, administrative, and service units—simultaneously distinctive from one another, yet responsive to one another in some fashion. In other words, our capacity for a networked rather than hierarchical structure allows for distinctiveness in the provision of reference and information services for the sciences, medicine, art, music, and the humanities and social sciences, yet these services are responsive to one another in planning, administration, and practice.

We hope to achieve organizational change by bringing together our colleagues who are responsible for the delivery of information services in an ongoing dialogue over policies and approaches to service and instruction, keeping in mind that what might be appropriate for one departmental library or service unit will not necessarily be fitting for another. A systemwide approach to reference that is sensitive to the loosely coupled nature of our campus is facilitated by the networking capabilities of information technologies.

> The old reality for reference at Iowa, as with most academic libraries, is that of a physical place.

OLD REALITIES

The old reality for reference at Iowa, as with most academic libraries, is that of a physical place. Our services were primarily focused on the desk as the center of information retrieval. We gave assistance to library patrons seeking information within the confines of our library, or, when not there, through interlibrary loan. Our public interface accommodated only information and reference assistance on demand. Library instruction was narrowly focused on the immediate needs of our users. The profession as a whole was unable to forecast the importance of teaching information-gathering skills for lifelong learning; that not all reference questions could be answered across a desk; nor the way in which new technologies and economic realities would push all libraries from ownership to access.

Our organizational structure supported function as a basis for library service. Structure based on function has a way of perpetuating the problem of walls between professional work. It does little to maximize participation or intellectual teamwork across the organization. Structure supporting function becomes a prohibiting factor in implementing anything that resembled Charles Martell's client-centered approach to information service, one in which the organization is structured around meeting the information needs of our academic communities and designed to improve the quality of work life for staff.

VISIONS

The turning point came when, just a few years ago before I arrived, both the Libraries and the University engaged in a major strategic planning initiative. At the University level, strategic planning meant identifying priorities in the academic program, incorporating concepts in cultural diversity, and focusing on undergraduate students. The Libraries' Strategic Plan calls for many specific initiatives. I have identified four key underlying assumptions in the plan that are pertinent:

- Greater integration of the University Libraries into the environment, the University community.
- Maximizing information technologies in gathering and delivering information.
- Reconceptualizing and expanding the educational objectives of the University Libraries.
- Integrating cultural diversity in our understanding of the Libraries' clientele and their information needs.

There are, of course, differences of opinion as to the effectiveness of strategic planning — in the management literature as well as inside many college and university library systems throughout the country. Yet for Iowa, our planning process — together with a self-assessment of our shared values and vision for the library's future — has helped us to take a concentric approach to information services. For instance, we can see that we have challenges in meeting information needs of undergraduate students through a web of information and instructional activities: user education delivered in a variety of settings and employing different technologies, reference on demand aided by emerging technologies, and individual and intensive consultation on research-oriented questions.

NEW REALITY

Based on our experiences, I see our new reality for reference as an organizational network of services. This is a concept that is consistent with flattening hierarchical structures in libraries, universities, corporations and other organizations. A network of reference and information services can accommodate consultation, on-demand assistance, and instruction as different, yet highly compatible nodes that are themselves distinctive yet responsive to one another. On-demand, once occupying a physical space in our old reality, can be distinguished from other modes of information provision by the concept of "point of use" rather than by the transaction across the desk. The desk can be retained as a hub for referral and "drop in" service; however, on-demand seeks alternative means for communicating queries. Alternate means of transmitting questions represents an important advancement in on-demand services. For instance, sending questions via electronic mail has tremendous potential for our user community. On-demand reference via electronic mail will give faculty, students, administrators, and others in the University community one more reason to activate their e-mail addresses. Presently we are involved in promoting electronic mail as a form of delivering information on our campus and, in particular, in using reference/information services. Ann Bristow recently noted in an article in C&RL News the success of electronic mail as a component of reference services at Indiana University. Bristow's "useful tips" include the following:

- "In order for reference service using e-mail to be generally useful it must be part of a larger electronic framework: a campus information system..."

- "The service will be used most by people who have integrated computing into all aspects of their work and communication."

These two points present us with one of our greater challenges — to work with our computing center, to make our electronic mail service a part of the emerging campus-information system. As a part of our contact with our clientele, whether through instruction, liaison relationships with academic programs, or our library-sponsored course on using the Internet, we are making them aware of how to activate accounts with our campus computing center, to use the Internet to search library catalogs, retrieve different sorts of information, and to use various lists and electronic discussions.

Research consultation services are highly compatible with on-demand services in the network of reference/information services because they present us with opportunities for short-term counseling. We receive many questions from our clientele that require us to create opportunities and an environment for more extensive interviews and dialogue between librarians and individual clients over research needs. Research consultations are opportunities in which we discuss potential electronic and print sources, map out strategies, and, when necessary, discuss methods of accessing information beyond our local collection. This includes the use of the Internet, electronic discussion lists, and information on how to obtain documents from (or travel to) other collections. The intent is not to actually do the research for the client, but to get them started on identifying information resources and to ensure that the client has the necessary skills to use those resources.

Yet another component of our network of reference/information services is the library's instruction program. Our program consists of more than course-related instructional activities. We have conducted research seminars for faculty and graduate students on the environment, women's studies, race and gender, Latino studies, Eastern Europe, and refugees. Some of these topics have been client driven as a result of surveys of past participants. Computer-Assisted Instruction has also become an area that represents a new reality for instructional programming. We've replaced group tours with a library video and program called Library Navigator, a hypertext program designed to introduce the Main Library and its services, providing hours and maps of the library system. Library Navigator is also being incorporated into the training program for new employees. Recently, we received an Instructional Computing

Award—the first non-academic department on our campus to do so— to develop a new CAI project called the Library Explorer that is aimed at undergraduate students, focusing on information sources and search tactics in the University Libraries. It will also include a segment on searching our online information system in that students will actually be able to simulate a search on our system. In addition, both our Health Sciences and Engineering Libraries are engaged in related projects. The head of the Engineering Library has begun to experiment with expert systems in the provision of basic information services.

There are three crucial reasons why what I have described as a new reality is fundamentally different from the old, changed by the vision for major revisions in reference/information services. First, I see this as shifting the physical concept of the "desk" as the basis for conducting reference service toward reference as a network of integrated information service activities. Reference is no longer constrained by a physical location. Instead, a networked approach to information services takes advantage of a variety of technologies. "Reference" can be conducted between clients and librarians, and among library staff on electronic mail, fax, or whatever alternative forms of communication exist. As Jerry Campbell recently stated, "our users themselves are gradually changing; they are coming to expect something different. They want information quickly, and they want it delivered to them. Increasingly they want it delivered in electronic form. Reference as we know it places a person between the public and the information." In effect, we are less concerned with document delivery than we are with information delivery.

Second, by conceptualizing reference/information services as a network of activities, we are able to circumvent the entire debate over where reference encounters should take place. Networked services are an alternative to hierarchical frameworks that elevate one type of service over another. Networked services also require us to define our services in such a way that *where* it is most appropriate to begin an information search process is clear to our clientele (and to our staff). For example, the concept of the research consultation is so rooted in the academic (i.e. faculty) model of one-on-one advising or counseling that it alone may be a poor substitute to reference on demand. This

...by conceptualizing reference/information services as a network of activities we are able to circumvent the entire debate over where reference encounters should take place.

is particularly true when it comes to meeting the information needs of undergraduate students.

Given our role as an academic support service, we need to employ a diversity of models that is compatible with our service orientation, which is to mesh information mediation with the educational process of information literacy. Networked information services can accomplish this by balancing needs at the point of use, consultation, and teaching through classrooms and through utilization of emerging technologies.

The third reason for developing a new reality is that most of the innovations reported in our literature have to do with maximizing the use of personnel. There are two dimensions to this issue. One has to do with the amount of staff we have available, given the fact that the days of growth are over for all of us. The other has to do with the utilization of professional expertise.

We can reallocate staff who perform other tasks to instructional development and reference consultations when they are not available for the desk. We are able to eliminate the walls that separate professional staff, which presents us with one of our most difficult challenges— because we are asking professionals to change the way they view their work. We also think that it is neither cost effective nor the best use of professional staff time to conduct tours, yet we realize that there's a perceived need for it. The development of Library Navigator has helped us decrease the amount of staff time devoted to tours while satisfying the needs of our clients for this kind of information. Also, utilizing staff from other departments such as technical services allows us to devote more time and energies to developing new strategies for the delivery of services. This kind of attention to the allocation of staff will promote the idea of partnerships with faculty on information-based projects. Again at Iowa, we hope to see this realized in large part through the Information Arcade, a multimedia, interactive information learning center in the Main Library designed to integrate library resources, new information technologies, and new concepts in teaching.

A NEW DEFINITION FOR REFERENCE

What will bring all of this together will be to redefine what we call reference. Jerry Campbell's controversial article, "Shaking the Conceptual Foundations of Reference: A Perspective," addresses just this point when he proposes that the term "reference" is outmoded; its connotations are obsolete. I am in agreement with Campbell on this point. Since my days as a library science student I have been uncomfortable with the term "reference," "reference librarian," etc. I felt that it was a term that people we sought to serve did not understand, and that it did not truly reflect the service that we were attempting to provide. The term "reference" was closely associated with the concept "bibliography," which described the book-centered nature of our profession circa 1930-1940. We can agree without argument that "bibliography" is an obsolete term that hardly describes the scope and depth of today's information services in academic libraries.

I have become an advocate in our Libraries to change the name of our department to Information and Instructional Services. I think that this will send a different message to our clientele and reflect more clearly our role as a mediating profession.

> Change means that we are venturing into partnerships with the rest of the university.

CONCLUSION

I am sure that the experiences I've conveyed are not unique to Iowa. The technologies that support our role as a profession residing between information and its users are changing so dramatically in a short period of time that our old realities cannot help but be confronted and changed. If we are attempting to view the provision of information services as a network of organizational responses to a mixture of information needs in the loosely coupled system of the university, we need to expand the definition, scope, and coverage of our interface with our clientele when engaged in handling information. We are challenged to move beyond the narrow constrictions of reference services as we used to know it.

At Iowa it means scaling away the idea that reference is a physical location and service is only performed on demand at the point of need. Change means that we are venturing into partnerships with the rest of the university to build more effective teams for advancing teaching and scholarship and networks for communicating needs and delivering information. From vision to reality is a continuous process of assessment and redesign, of letting go of old ideas and trying new innovations.

SOURCES

Bristow, Ann. Academic Reference Service Over Electronic Mail. *C&RL News* 53: 631-637 (November 1992)

Campbell, Jerry D. Shaking the Conceptual Foundations of Reference: a Perspective. *Reference Services Review* 20: 29-36 (Winter 1992)

Cargill, Jennifer. The Electronic Reference Desk: Reference Service in an Electronic World. *Library Administration and Management*

Orton, J; Douglas and Karl E. Weick. The Loosely Coupled Systems: a Reconceptualization. *The Academy of Management Review* 15: 203-23 (April 1990)

8 • TOTAL CHANGE AT THE UNIVERSITY OF ARIZONA

Karen Williams
Social Sciences Team Leader
University of Arizona Library, Tucson

I intend to tease you today with a five-minute infomercial about the changes at the University of Arizona, and hope that you will choose to attend one of the soapbox sessions on this topic tomorrow. The University of Arizona Library is currently undergoing a complete restructuring. The process began in February of 1992 and has been divided into several phases. To date, a little more than half of the librarians and career staff have been directly involved with the process by serving on one of the many planning teams. All other staff have had opportunities to contribute comments and ideas through a series of open houses and all-staff meetings.

The first question on everyone's mind is why are we doing this? The several reasons in a nutshell include technological advances that make it possible to offer whole new services and conduct business very differently; the information explosion, which makes it impossible for research libraries to even pretend to own everything of value to their clienteles; the fact that traditional organization structures better serve formats than patrons; and the pervasive budget cuts that higher education is experiencing as the public calls for better service and more accountability. The University of Arizona is engaged in a campus-wide program of assessment and evaluation called Continuous Organizational Renewal, or CORe, providing us with a great framework for our work. We really believe that it is necessary for all of us in the library profession to re-examine the way we do business in light of all of these changes. The restructuring was not driven solely by budget cuts. We did not set out to restructure using the Total Quality Management, or TQM, methods, but when we looked at what we had come up with, there were many iden-

> The old organization had four division heads and sixteen department heads. The new organization has no division heads and eight team leaders. The goal of a team leader is to eventually work yourself out of a job.

tifiable TQMesque principles. The Restructuring Steering Committee articulated a number of priorities and assumptions for the new organization which I will summarize here:

- We are committed to quality.
- By reorganizing, we can increase productivity and gain efficiencies.
- Needs assessment and connection development are essential. We will be proactive, not reactive.
- We will remain flexible to meet the changing needs of our clientele.
- It is our goal to empower patrons and help them become self-sufficient to the greatest extent possible.
- We will reduce hierarchy in the organization. Staff will be empowered to make decisions at the appropriate level.
- Staff will be involved in designing and improving services and processes.
- Data will be used for decision making.
- Risk taking is encouraged.
- Education and staff development are vital.
- We must form partnerships on campus and with other appropriate groups.
- We will use whole systems thinking, rather than turf orientation.
- Cooperation, not competition.

What are some of the most radical changes? The equivalent of public services teams are, for the most part, subject based rather than format based. There are three types of reference service: Type 1 includes Information Desks which handle quick-answer and directional questions. These desks will be staffed by library assistant classifications and library school students. Type 2 is very similar to traditional reference service, except that we will not attempt to handle more sophisticated or longer inquiries here. Type 2 desks are staffed by a team which includes one librarian serving as lead person, and either two staff (Library Specialist or Library Supervisor), or one staff and one Library School student. Type 3 service is one on one, or reference by appointment. Questions received at a Type 2 desk that cannot adequately be addressed there will be referred to the appropriate subject specialist by handing out business cards. The Undergraduate Services Team is responsible for the coordination of the service desks. All other teams must contribute 20% of their total staff time to Undergraduate Services for staffing desks and assistance with general instruction and projects.

The key work activities of the integrative services teams (public services) include education, connection development, information resource development/preservation, needs assessment, type 3 reference service, and knowledge management. The new organization is team based. Team leaders will replace department heads. All team leaders report directly to the Dean. The old organization had four division heads and sixteen department heads. The new organization has no division heads and eight team leaders. The goal of a team leader is to eventually work yourself out of a job.

All team leader positions will be open internally to all qualified candidates; no former department heads are automatically placed in team leader positions. A Selection Committee was formed, chaired by the Dean and including four elected librarians and four elected career staff. Once team leaders have been selected, all other librarians and career staff will complete a Critical Skills/Abilities/Knowledge Checklist and will be reassigned into the new organizational structure.

Our target date for having the teams in place is the end of July, 1993. It has been an incredibly exciting and exhausting year and a half. We are looking forward to the future.

9 • REFERENCE SERVICES IN AN ON-LINE ENVIRONMENT: SOME IMPLICATIONS FOR STAFFING

Larry R. Oberg
University Librarian
Willamette University, Salem, Oregon

REDEFINING REFERENCE

Librarians today are deeply immersed in the process of redefining academic library reference services. Several bifurcated models have emerged that separate the questions posed by our clientele by level of complexity. In these models, the less complex questions are answered by students or support staff and the more complex questions are referred to librarian specialists for advanced consultation.

NEW MODELS

A number of reasons account for why these new service models have appeared. One important reason is because reference and instruction librarians are now using, and teaching the use of, the growing number of on-line information resources available through the global Internet. This is a new role for reference librarians and it contrasts sharply with their more clearly defined traditional mission of selecting and storing in-house a limited number of print resources from which they retrieved with relative ease the information required by their patrons.

Clearly, the Internet is affecting profoundly what these librarians do and how they do it. It also changes the work habits, the perceived needs, and the expectations of researchers. It is likely that more questions will come to be posed over the networks than across the reference desk and more of the information desired by our clients will be available through the Internet than in our traditional print collections. "Because of the proliferation of information sources," Malinconico points out, "users will be in greater, rather than lesser, need of information assistance." [1]

> One way in which we have managed to cope with this change is through the delegation to support staff of many complex and challenging tasks that were once performed more or less exclusively by librarians.

A PATTERN OF CHANGE

The paradigm shift that many of us expect to see in reference, indeed, in public services generally, is part of a broad spectrum of rapid change within academic libraries that has been occurring for the past twenty or more years. One way in which we have managed to cope with this change is through the delegation to support staff of many complex and challenging tasks that were once performed more or less exclusively by librarians. The enormity of the change in the utilization and deployment of library staff is most evident in technical services where paraprofessionals have come to dominate both cataloging and acquisitions.[2] Indeed, out of this process, a new category of employee, the paraprofessional, has emerged.

The accelerating use of paraprofessionals to perform tasks once considered professional allows librarians to concentrate more of their time upon their higher-level responsibilities. For example, by picking up the slack, support staff made it possible for librarians to assume their faculty-status obligations of research, teaching, and governance. They will also make it possible for us to implement a new model of reference services. Parenthetically, it may be thanks to support staff that some of you managed to get away to be here at Duke today!

In my opinion, we will see another major shift of tasks from librarians to support staff as we construct the new reference model. The use of support staff in reference, however, will be quantitatively different from our past practice of pressing graduate students and support staff into service merely to spell librarians for meetings and database searching. The new models of reference service that exist at Johns Hopkins, Brandeis,[3] Arizona State West, and elsewhere are grounded firmly in the concept of an information desk staffed exclusively by support staff or students. It is likely that these categories of employees will become responsible for answering considerably more than fifty percent of the reference questions posed in most academic libraries.

Given the enormity of the changes that I expect to see occur, it seemed to me that it would be useful to briefly review the traditional criteria that defines a profession and remind you of some of the problems that have been created by the recent massive shift of tasks and responsibilities from librarians to support staff. I will conclude by suggesting that the changes in reference we all expect to be instrumental in bringing about offer us an opportunity to define more clearly than we have done in the past the roles of both support staff and librarians.

WHAT IS A PROFESSION?

Today, the noun profession tends to be used interchangeably with the adjective professional. This linguistic slight-of-hand allows everyone in this society, if they work hard and make an honest living, to call themselves professional. The traditional definition of a profession and its practitioners is quite different and, whether we accept that definition, reject it, or wish to change it, we should at the least be familiar with it. For, as we move toward a new model of reference, we will inevitably strengthen or weaken librarianship, at least in reference to its classic definition.

For the past one hundred years or more, it has been assumed that a continuum exists between the crafts and the professions. Criteria defining professions were established early on and, surprisingly, they have changed little over time. All occupations can be ranked along this continuum and the closer they approach the professional end of the spectrum, the more professional they are presumed to be.

An early and classic enunciation of the criteria by which aspiring professions may be judged is Abraham Flexner's famous 1915 consideration of the relative professional merits of social work.[4] Most formulations that followed were derivative of Flexner's pioneering effort, an effort that was to influence profoundly several generations of librarians.

By 1961, Ralph M. Edwards could abstract six criteria from his reading of the literature that had accumulated since Flexner's time.[5] They are:

> The criteria used to distinguish librarians, paraprofessionals, technicians, telecommunications and computer specialists, and others have become, in fact, frighteningly blurred.

1. A profession possesses a body of knowledge and systematically organized theory that is essential to the performance of the service it provides. Practitioners are expected to contribute to that body of knowledge.

2. A profession provides services that are both important to society and a matter of broad public concern.

3. Because of the superior knowledge and competence of its practitioners, society grants a profession a monopoly on the right to perform its services and to establish criteria for admitting new members to its ranks.

4. Because of the superior knowledge of its members, no one outside of the profession is qualified to exercise authority over, or evaluate the quality of, the services provided.

5. Because society defers to the authority of professionals and grants them a monopoly over their practice, it is incumbent upon professionals to establish a stringent self-regulating code of ethics, in which the good of society takes precedent over personal benefit.

6. The individual members of the profession form a distinct professional culture, are motivated by altruism, profess responsibility to society, and take pride in the profession's accomplishments. Professional identification is central to the life and self concept of the professional.

This definition, or something closely akin, has been the yardstick by which librarians have measured their personal development and that of their occupation for nearly a hundred years. I leave it to you to speculate on how closely librarianship approaches this classic model. When professions were attacked as elitist in the 1960s, our response was to jettison the authoritarian model of administration in favor of a consensus-based model and to organize ourselves collegially rather than hierarchically. Ironically, both of these democratic changes strengthen librarianship when it is measured against the criteria of professionalism.

ROLE BLURRING

Since we began upgrading support staff, however, we have seemed less and less able to define with precision the boundaries that separate categories of employees within our libraries and, indeed, within our computer centers. Hence, who and what is professional has become blurred. My reading is that we are uncomfortable with this ambiguity. Should we feel threatened? Can we expect to define professional and nonprofessional roles unambiguously in the current climate, at least in a way that, as Ann Boyer says, would "remain valid over time?" Or, as she puts it, is our desire for neat categories of employees merely "othering?"[6]

Othering is not the problem, in my opinion, and I think that we should be concerned. The criteria used to distinguish librarians, paraprofessionals, technicians, telecommunications and computer specialists, and others have become, in fact, frighteningly blurred. Role blurring is damaging in many ways. It weakens us as a profession. For example, it devalues librarians in the eyes of their clientele who may doubt their expertise and be reluctant to accept them as colleagues.

Role blurring has created considerable discontent within the ranks of the support staff. Because we now expect support staff to assume tasks they have watched librarians perform for years, not to mention many challenging new tasks created by automation, they feel cheated, under-paid, underclassified, and undervalued. Their frustration manifests itself in many ways. Increasingly, they challenge the MLS as an irrelevant and unnecessary barrier to advancement. They also demand — quite rightly it seems to me — that more notice of them be taken, and they emphasize their need for increased opportunities for staff development, travel, and inclusion in the decision-making process.

REDEEMING THE PROFESSION

This profound change in our traditional staffing patterns has oc-curred at the grass roots, unfettered by such niceties as leadership, critical analysis, or standards and guidelines elaborated by our associations. I consider this a dereliction of, dare I say, our professional obligation. Because ignoring the problem not only weakens librarianship, it also prevents us from playing fair with support staff. Although individual libraries and library systems may have created equitable environments, all too many are weighted down with outmoded, often counterproductive, staffing structures. This allows us to continue to exploit those who bring unique capabilities and qualifications to jobs that do not require certifi-cation or standardized degree requirements.

Poised, as we now are, on the brink of a paradigm shift of unprec-edented proportions, we have the opportunity to redeem librarianship by self-consciously addressing the problems of staff utilization and deploy-ment in a rapidly changing environment. Unambiguously defined catego-ries of employees may continue to elude us, but we can do better. Not to come to grips with a rapidly deteriorating staffing situation weakens librarianship, regardless of whether you consider our field a traditional profession or merely a craft. The reconfiguration of reference services offers us the best opportunity we may ever have to seize the initiative in this important arena.

REFERENCES

1. S. Michael Malinconico, "What Librarians Need to Know to Survive in an Age of Technology," *Education for Library and Information Science,* v.33, no.3, Summer 1992, 239.

2. Oberg reports that more than 90 percent of the ARL libraries assign copy cataloging to paraprofessionals, more than 50 percent assign original descriptive cataloging to them, and 36 percent assign them subject analysis and classification. See Larry R. Oberg et al., "The Role, Status, and Working Conditions of Paraprofessionals: A National Survey of Academic Libraries," *College & Research Libraries* v.53, no.3, May 1992, 225.

3. See Virginia Massey-Burzio, "Reference Encounters of a Different Kind: A Symposium," *The Journal of Academic Librarianship,* v.18, no.5, November 1992, 276-286.

4. Abraham Flexner, "Is Social Work a Profession?" *School and Society,* v.1, June 1915, 901-911.

5. Ralph M. Edwards, *The Role of the Beginning Librarian in the University of California Libraries.* DLS dissertation, Berkeley, School of Library and Information Studies, University of California 1971, 60-62.

6. Ann Boyer, "Letter to the Editor," *College & Research Libraries* v.54, no.1, January 1993, 74.

10 • ISLANDS IN A SEA OF CHANGE

James Rettig

Assistant University Librarian for Reference and Information Services
College of William and Mary, Williamsburg, Virginia

Visions—other, perhaps, than visions of grandeur—do not often come to members of the American Library Association's Council during that body's sometimes contentious meetings. However, in June of 1991 in Atlanta during an ALA Council session, a vision came to me. Two weeks earlier I had learned that I had been elected vice-president/president-elect of ALA's Reference and Adult Services Division. The idle rumination I had engaged in while a candidate about what I, as RASD president, might emphasize and bring to reference librarians' attention had taken on gravity and urgency. In the aftermath of the closing of the Columbia University School of Library Service, ALA had appointed a task force to study the library education crisis and make recommendations. Russell Shank, chair of that task force, was presenting his report to the Council. He concluded by quoting Jesse Shera:

> I described changes, especially changes driven by technology, in the environment in which reference service operates; I made the case that these changes form an imperative for rethinking and redefining reference.

> As I see it, the great need of the library profession today is to formulate a professional philosophy that will meet the rapidly changing needs of society for recorded knowledge. We must re-define our role in society, emphasizing new functions and new services that will make of the library the agency it should be in the total communication process. Such a reassessment relates to every aspect of library services from those directed to the preschool child to those assigned primarily for the scientist and scholar.

This struck a responsive chord in me and it became clear to me that my focus as RASD president would be on rethinking reference. My good fortune to be elected RASD president and the opportunities it presented —writing four columns in *RQ* on issues in reference librarianship and planning the RASD program at the 1993 annual conference—happily coincided with rising recognition throughout the profession of a need to redefine the premises on which reference and information services rest and a growing conviction that we must deliver those services in new ways.

I was able to raise these issues publicly a year later in my first president's column in *RQ*.[2] In that column I quoted the decisive passage above from Shera as well as Frederick Kilgour's comment to the OCLC User's Council in June, 1991, that "Thinking about libraries in 2001 can be a comfortable self-deception; you don't have to do anything now. But if libraries don't do something now, someone else will." I described changes, especially changes driven by technology, in the environment in which reference service operates; I made the case that these changes form an imperative for rethinking and redefining reference. I concluded that column with a call (indeed, a stirring call, or so I believed) to reference librarians in all types of libraries to share with me informal reports of their innovations and their efforts to redefine reference. I promised to share this information in the Spring, 1993, *RQ*. Then I waited for the responses to pour in. And I waited...and I waited...and I waited.

The one response I received was welcome, even if not germane to the questions I raised. It put me back in touch with a man who graduated from my high school two years ahead of me and who, unbeknownst to me, has worked for a number of years as a reference librarian at the Library of Congress.

FOUR TRENDS

So what I offer you is not the report I envisioned and promised in *RQ*, but the observations of a passionately interested observer of—and participant in—the effort to retool reference service.[3] Thanks to the ongoing conversation carried on through the LIBREF-L listserv provided by the reference staff at Kent State University, thanks to scattered reports in the journal literature, and thanks to my contacts in the field (especially among academic libraries), I was able to solicit responses from librarians at those libraries I identified as actively involved in some way in the redefinition process. I was also able to categorize those responses into four groups.

Tiered service structures: The innovation that has stirred the most interest is tiered reference structures. These are sometimes assigned the rubric of "doing away with the reference desk." A tiered reference structure attempts to channel users' questions to a central service point staffed,

78

generally, by paraprofessionals. They answer and thereby filter out routine questions and refer others' questions to professionals. The Brandeis and Johns Hopkins changes in this direction have been reported here earlier today as well as in the journal literature.[4] Such systems differentiate levels of service and differentiate the roles and responsibilities of paraprofessional and professional staff.

Floating reference librarians: This is an effort to get the reference librarian out from behind the desk. The librarians spend at least part of their time while on "desk duty" (or its equivalent) ranging among users as they interact with information sources (especially an OPAC or CD-ROM systems). The floating (or "roving") reference librarians observe the users and routinely inquire if they would like assistance. They also intervene when they observe a user foundering or wandering about. Boston College has experimented extensively and, reportedly, very successfully with this mode of service.

Going out to users: A step beyond "floating" reference service are efforts to go out to users in their native habitats – their campus offices and laboratories. For the next year or two Curtin University in Perth, Australia, has assigned a librarian to one of that university's four academic divisions. This librarian is responsible for diagnosing faculty members' information needs, providing counsel on information management, offering training in information retrieval, and establishing channels between the library and the faculty to provide optimum access to local and worldwide information resources. The McFarlin Library at the University of Tulsa plans to develop three similar positions—one for each of that university's three colleges. In addition to the duties noted for the Curtin position, these positions will have responsibility for bibliographic instruction and collection assessment. Tulsa sees these as something different from subject specialist or collection development positions. The purpose of such efforts is to get to know users and their needs better and to help users learn how they can fulfill those needs even when they are outside the library facility.

User studies: Some libraries are undertaking formal efforts to get to know their users—their erstwhile users, their potential users, and the needs of all of these people. The library at the Massachusetts Institute of Technology has taken an in-depth look at the information needs of three groups. Hand-in-hand with this effort is a year-long re-examination by the managers of the library's various public service units of the ways in which reference services are offered.[6]

My solicitations to librarians developing information and finding tools employing artificial intelligence proved for naught; the only response I received indicated that the program I asked about had been discontinued when the person to whom I had addressed my letter left that institution. Nevertheless, reference librarians' growing interest in artificial intelligence systems may be furthered by emerging, and thus far still experimental, administrative mergers of libraries and computer centers.

TWO CALLS, TWO DIFFERENCT RESPONSES

All of these trends and efforts burgeon with promise. Yet two things strike me about the ways in which I learned of them. First, reports of some were published and widely disseminated so that others could learn about them. However, others were mentioned in passing as a part of responses to various issues under discussion on a listserv. These and other efforts, unreported and undiscovered (at least by me), stand as islands in a sea of change. We need better reporting mechanisms for sharing information about our experiments. And we need to evaluate those experiments rigorously and report the results of those assessments boldly, allowing the chips to fall where they will. Second, I wonder what difference the way in which a call for information is posed makes. In *RQ* I invited readers to "Tell me about the innovative service programs you have devised; share with me your ideas about how reference and adult services ought to change, either by evolution or revolution; tell me your dreams for the reference and adult services of the future; tell me what trends you see transforming the environment in which we function; tell me how you think libraries and librarians will interact with the environment of the future; but most of all, please tell me how you and your colleagues are already transforming the services you offer to meet the challenges of a changing environment."[7]

In September of 1991 Anne Lipow had posted a query on LIBADMIN asking how reference departments are reorganizing. Her posting elicited twenty times as many responses as did my call in *RQ*. Did the specificity of her query with its focus on "reorganization" have an effect on the response? Or was it simply that response by e-mail is so easy that people availed themselves of that opportunity? I offered *RQ's* readers the opportunity to respond by e-mail, but outside the interactive environment of the listserv, it seems that either this was not convenient enough or that the call for information was posed in a way that readers did not link their efforts to the broader issues. (As president of the association that publishes it, I understandably hesitate to suggest that *RQ* simply isn't read.) Could it be that we are more comfortable with an issue when it is couched in practical terms rather than in a broader context? All of Anne Lipow's respondents and all but one of the libraries I was able to report on are academic libraries. To a certain extent this reflects the current state of Internet access among libraries. However it may also indicate that the ferment has begun in academic library reference departments but has yet to spill over in any significant way to other types of libraries. If this is indeed the case, this conference offers significant opportunities for its participants to provide leadership to the entire profession.

EMPHASIS ON INDIVIDUAL USERS

The common thread running through the experiments to redefine reference service is a renewed and refreshing emphasis on the needs of individual users. Tiered service, floating reference, outreach efforts, and user studies all are intended to meet user needs as they arise one at a time in disparate individuals. However, as Jerry Campbell has pointed out, it is "not feasible from the standpoint of library budgets to provide enough staff members to offer face-to-face answers as the number of reference questions"[8] and individual information needs escalate. And as more and more information services become available around the clock, the pressure to provide that sort of service becomes potentially non-stop. To compound matters, the new information services increase both the complexity and the number of options information seekers face, thus increasing the likelihood that they will need assistance to assure success. Campbell has suggested that the computer offers promise for solving this dilemma; and he entrusts to reference librarians (renamed Access Engineers in his nomenclature[9]) major responsibility for mapping the information landscape, for studying user needs, and for engineering the transfer of information from its source(s) to users when and where they need it.

One could argue that the mechanisms for this last task already exist to a considerable extent. It is easy enough, especially for members of most academic institutions, to connect to the Internet and its mind-boggling array of information sources. Once connected, all of those resources are

...the new information services increase both the complexity and the number of options information seekers face, thus increasing the likelihood that they will need assistance to assure success.

81

available for nearly instant transfer to one's hard drive. But...it just isn't that simple. The Internet has developed (I hesitate to say "has been designed") without the benefit of significant influence from the principles of ergonomics. It suffers mightily from a malady called "the complexity problem," which ergonomic engineer Charles Mauro has defined as "a fundamental mismatch between the demands of a technology and the capabilities of its user."[10] The universally acknowledged worst-case example of the complexity problem is the programmable VCR. Were OPACs and CD-ROM database search systems as ubiquitous in homes as are VCRs, they rather than VCRs might be the object of comedians' jokes and consumers' ire. Vice-President Gore's vision for the NREN will come to naught if NREN does not solve the complexity problem better than the Internet has. FTP, archie, and even the relatively user-friendly veronica require training; none functions in an intuitively self-evident way. The presence of a "dense instruction manual" accompanying a device or system is, in Mauro's judgment, "the clearest sign of design failure."[11] Thus, the recent outpouring of useful how-to books explaining the use of the Internet signifies that from the user's perspective the Internet's design is a failure, even if it is also a remarkable engineering feat.

> Thus the recent outpouring of useful how-to books explaining the use of the Internet signifies that from the user's perspective the Internet's design is a failure, even if it is also a remarkable engineering feat.

FUTURE ROLES FOR REFERENCE LIBRARIANS

The Internet, our OPACs, and our CD-ROM search systems cry out for what ergonomic engineers call "user-centered design."[12] Devices and systems created through effective user-centered design not only maximize simplicity and ease of use, they "also enhance a worker's feeling of control instead of depriving him of it."[13] Whether we call ourselves reference librarians or Access Engineers, we need to be deeply involved—from inception to product delivery—in the development of the information systems that will allow users to expedite information transfer without a librarian's mediation. We must be involved (as, of course, must representative users) in designing systems that will both meet users' diverse individual needs and satisfy the routine queries that today account for so many of our reference desk transactions.

One way in which a good reference librarian adds value to an individual's information seeking is by helping the individual articulate and refine that need. In order to replicate this valuable function, automated systems need to be designed so they are almost conversational. This is where our knowledge of the information landscape can be invaluable. Greater cooperation between systems engineers, both in the commercial and the not-for-profit sectors, and librarians ought to result in systems that are more user-centered, systems that free librarians from the repetition and routine of the reference desk so they can study users' needs and work to assure the speedy, easy transfer of information to users when and where they need it.

PAST AND FUTURE

As we work to invent and shape the future, we dare not lose sight of the past. Some of the experiments being tried today have antecedents; they echo efforts recounted in Rothstein's history of reference service to mid-century or later efforts reported elsewhere.[14] However, just as not all of today's experiments are being reported as widely nor in as timely a fashion as is desirable, many of the past's experiments were probably never reported. And one wonders how many were judged failures and not reported for that reason. Nevertheless, when designing new structures or initiatives, we would do well to review the literature stored in our libraries for use in just such situations and to learn what we can from the experiments of the past. At the same time we need to think of posterity. We must forthrightly report the results of our experiments and disseminate them widely; in this way we can, perhaps, save future generations from reinventing the wheels we are crafting today. We cannot afford insularity amidst this vast sea of change in the information environment. Only by sharing information on these initiatives and their success or failure and analyzing the reasons for successes and for failures will we be able to discern (or, perhaps, reaffirm) the principles on which librarians can build service programs designed to meet clients' needs.

We live in a time of change. Technological change is a constant in our professional lives. Inherent in that change lies a message for librarianship. Similarly, the electorate endorsed national political change last November. That change made explicit a message that affects library workers along with the rest of the nation — "Don't stop thinkin' about tomorrow. Don't stop; it'll soon be here. It'll be here better than before. Yesterday's gone; yesterday's gone."

REFERENCES

1. Jesse H. Shera, "Formulate a Professional Philosophy." in "Diagnosis." *Library Journal* 88 (January 1, 1963): 50.

2. James Rettig, "Rethinking Reference and Adult Services." *RQ* 31 (Summer 1992): 463-6.

3. James Rettig, "Rethinking Reference and Adult Services: A Preliminary Report." *RQ* 32 (Spring 1993): 310-14.

4. Virginia Massey-Burzio, "Reference Encounters of a Different Kind: A Symposium." *Journal of Academic Librarianship* 18 (November 1992): 276-86.

5. Adeane Bregman and Barbara Mento, "Reference Roving at Boston College" *College and Research Libraries News* 53 (November 1992): 634-37.

6. *Information Services Study, Final Report.* Cambridge, MA: MIT Libraries, October 1992.

7. Rettig, "Rethinking Reference and Adult Services," 466.

8. Jerry D. Campbell, "Shaking the Conceptual Foundations of Reference: A Perspective." *Reference Services Review* 20 (Winter 1992): 30.

9. ibid., 32.

10. John Sedgwick, "The Complexity Problem." *Atlantic* 271 (March 1993): 96.

11. ibid., 98.

12. ibid., 96-104.

13. ibid., 103.

14. Samuel Rothstein. *The Development of Reference Services through Academic Traditions, Public Library Practice, and Special Librarianship.* Chicago: Association of College and Reference Libraries, 1955.

NEW DIRECTIONS

BRAINSTORMING THE FUTURE

11. NEW REFERENCE MODELS

12. PRACTICAL NEXT STEPS: HOW TO GET WHERE WE WANT TO GO

This chapter contains the consolidated outcomes of the small groups' work at Berkeley and Duke, respectively. The specific instructions to the small groups for fulfilling each task can be found in Appendix D.

In small groups, participants completed two tasks:

Task #1: *Identify the components of a new reference model—both what new will emerge and what current components will decline or disappear.*

Then, after airing and consolidating the results of Task #1,

Task #2: *Consider what changes will be required to implement the new model and suggest practical steps that staff can take to implement the changes.*

11. NEW REFERENCE MODELS

BERKELEY: SMALL GROUP TASK #1

PART 1.
EMERGING AND DESIRABLE CHARACTERISTICS AND COMPONENTS

ORGANIZATIONAL STRUCTURES
1. Teams, collaborative workgroups
2. Job rotation, cross training
3. Partnerships (faculty, computer center, other expertise on campus)
4. Flattening hierarchy
5. Empowerment
6. Increased accountability
7. Maintain "dual" role (print and electronic)
8. User-centered (informed by user studies)
9. Decentralized/remote service

SERVICES
1. Remote users
2. Electronic service delivery
3. "Tiered" reference service
    (Continuum from self-service —> desk —> consultation by appointment)
4. On-demand information delivery, independent of time and place
5. Librarian involvement in creating custom user tools with intuitive interfaces
6. Reduced desk hours
7. Rovers
8. Document delivery
9. Marketing reference services
10. Targeted services for specific clienteles
11. Collection development moving toward resource management
12. Outreach
13. Proactive
14. More access/less ownership
15. One-stop shopping

DUKE: SMALL GROUP TASK #1

PART 1.

EMERGING AND DESIRABLE CHARACTERISTICS AND COMPONENTS

ORGANIZATIONAL STRUCTURE
- team oriented
- from local to regional structure
- collaborative decision-making
- more staff with split responsibility
- client centered
- more empowered department heads
- decentralized/interdepartmental
- external focus
- flattened, flexible and fluid
- alliances with computer centers
- consolidate service points
- more variety in department structures
- participatory
- incorporation of users into organizational structure
- collegial model

SERVICES
- deliver information in user defined form
- information packaging
- provide services on users' terms with evaluation
- outreach
- market research
- quality filtering
- more computer-aided-instruction
- alternate funding sources (for services)
- increasingly equipment dependent
- collaboration with other professionals
- proactive locally and nationally
- more value-added services
- tiered services
    from on-demand to appointment
    from help screens to command mode
- self-service
- client-centered/client controlled
- emphasize end-user searching
- pre-packaged BI

BERKELEY: SMALL GROUP TASK #1

STAFFING
1. Electronic resources librarian
2. Rovers
3. More flexible job assignments (including telecommuting)
4. Residencies and internships
5. Increased use of paraprofessionals, students
6. Temporary librarians
7. Analytical/critical thinking
8. Information creators
9. More specialization
10. More technological sophistication
11. Ongoing continuing education, training
12. Reallocation of staff to reference
13. Remote office hours
14. Higher level skills
15. Wider variety of acceptable degrees (not just the MLS)
16. "Graying" professional corps
17. More diverse staff

TOOLS AND EQUIPMENT
1. Networked workstations
2. Internet/NREN
3. Equipment for persons with disabilities
4. Multimedia and hypermedia
5. Electronic information desks
6. Document delivery equipment
7. Optical scanning/transmitting
8. Flexible workspace
9. Tools (software) for analysis
10. Videophone
11. Technological infrastructure (e.g., CWIS)
12. Expert systems
13. Fewer print resources
14. Co-development with vendor

DUKE: SMALL GROUP TASK #1

STAFFING
- less staff
- more diverse
- ongoing staff training
- expertise
  tech/computer
  higher level
  subject
  library
- fuller roles for all levels of support staff
- shorter desk hours
- more generalists
- continually redefine "ref." roles
- service orientation
- more r & d

TOOLS AND EQUIPMENT
- user interface
  standard (international?)
  user-driven
  flexible
- one information gateway/universal workstation
- intuitive systems — "no manual required"
- librarian participation in system design
- less dependence on location
- LANs and other networks
- multimedia workstations
- trouble free (robust) equipment
- inevitability of changing tools
- more resource sharing
- shift from ownership to access

BERKELEY: SMALL GROUP TASK #1

CLIENTELE
1. Remote users (campus, local, state, international)
2. More sophisticated users/needs
3. More diverse e.g., ethnic, nontraditional, international; primary (students, faculty, staff), secondary (students of other institutions, community users, alums, affiliate users); different levels of skill
4. More business (fee paying and free)
5. Have greater expectations
6. More demanding
7. Technologically naive
8. Less patient
9. More self-sufficient

UNRESOLVED ISSUES
1. Fee or free ?
2. More or less staff ?
3. More or less bibliographic instruction ?
4. Form and substance of BI ?
5. More or less group or individual BI ?

DUKE: SMALL GROUP TASK #1

CLIENTELE
- more remote users (global)
- higher user expectations/more demanding
- diverse needs
- changing demographic user profile
- more computer literate
- more service for info. have-nots
- ADA concerns get more attention
- client status determines service level

FACILITIES (NEW CATEGORY)
- renovated
- flexible
- adaptable
- heavily wired

UNRESOLVED ISSUE
- more or less bibliographic instruction?

BERKELEY: SMALL GROUP TASK NO. 1

PART 2. DECLINING AND DISAPPEARING SERVICES

1. Long and customized bibliographies, guides and pathfinders
2. Printed indexes/sources
3. Mediated online searching
4. MLS at the desk
5. Reference librarians at desk
6. Some service points, including branches
7. Administrative layers
8. Duplicate formats
9. Staffing allocation in technical services
10. Staff answering low-level questions
11. Equal service for non-primary clientele
12. Interlibrary loan verification at reference desks
13. Collection development responsibility
14. Written reference correspondence
15. Index tables
16. Elaborate vertical files
17. Custom computer guides
18. Orientation, tours
19. Telephone service
20. Double coverage at reference desk
21. Reference desk hours
22. Evening and weekend desk hours
23. Full MARC cataloging

DUKE: SMALL GROUP TASK NO. 1

PART 2. DECLINING AND DISAPPEARING SERVICES

- eliminate duplicate services elsewhere on campus
- stop excessive local customization
- preparation of bibliographies
- decrease duplication of print and electronic resources
- mediated services
- mediated ILL
- building tours
- all-purpose desk
- librarian performance of clerical tasks
- cut out/pare down management activities
- MLS-staffed reference desks/departments
- "sit and wait" reference model
- give up library as a place
- paper-based peripheral collections
- hours of staffed service
- front-line reference librarians
- less "how to"/more "why" BI.
- no BI (?)

12. PRACTICAL NEXT STEPS: HOW TO GET WHERE WE WANT TO GO

BERKELEY: SMALL GROUP TASK #2

Develop new roles
- Increased use of paraprofessional students
- More user needs assessment
- Generate data about current environment
- Develop pilot program with librarians working in situ
- Increased use of paraprofessionals at desk
- Develop guidelines
- Determine appropriate classification
- Allocate funds/equipment
- Develop a training program. Components:
    a) Modules/CAI
    b) Observation of other staff
    c) Assignments/feedback
    d) Videotaping/role playing
    e) Release time

Redefine reference to make it more responsive to clients
- Needs assessment
    a) Focus groups—users/staff
    b) Outside mediator, facilitator
    c) User study
    d) Statistical analyses
- Examine titles
- Redefine staff roles
- Reassess information belief systems

Increase availability of modes of remote access
(more modes, better utilization, support, equipment, training)
- Survey user preferences (proficiency, equipment, fees)
- Work with campus partners
    a) e-mail access, equipment for all primary clientele
    b) user interfaces/templates for e-mail reference, etc.

Integrate Internet resources information svc repertory
(both librarians' and users')
- Identify campus training resources
- Develop staff training
- Provide training for faculty, users
- Install public Internet workstations in library
- Incorporate Internet into handouts, BI, reference exchanges

DUKE: SMALL GROUP TASK #2

Computerized/networked electronic ACCESS to information for all users
- Base decisions on user analysis/market research
  Contact experts in academic departments (e.g., marketing, sociology)
- Invite vendor representatives to discuss issues/trends
- Initiate discussion with computer center

Ongoing staff development at all levels
- Share results of "Rethinking"
- Free up staff time for experimenting with/learning new information products
- Work on building consensus on issues and sharing knowledge and ideas

Change organizational and physical structures
- Eliminate ONE administrative level (e.g., AUL)
- Encourage/force "roving" reference librarian. (e.g., forbid reference librarians to sit at desk for a week)
- Make contacts with physical facilities staff or experts on campus

Cultivate changes in attitude
- Establish common institutional values; use consultant to help clarify values
- Establish common ground rules for individual and group behavior

Free librarians' time for higher level tasks
- Assess use of reference desk
- Assess how many & what level staff are needed
- Identify tasks & conduct workload studies
- Simplify processes
- Eliminate duplication of effort

Eliminate duplication of materials and services to maximize resources
- Develop a strategy to identify duplicate services and materials
- Undertake partner alliances and consumer analysis
- Establish communication with campus units
- Establish priorities and responsibility for services

Develop the expertise of "the team" to create a staff in which individuals have areas of technical and subject specialization.
- Identify strengths and needs of present staff
- Retrain, hire, and rewrite job descriptions

BERKELEY: SMALL GROUP TASK #2

Promote opportunities for in-depth reference
- Keep business cards of subject specialists at reference desk for referral
- Include subsequent reference encounters in reference statistics
- Keep and publicize office hours
- Develop subject-oriented expert systems

Meet users where they are, when they need
- Identify and attend dept. mtgs and seminars
- Make appts, keep office hrs. in departments
- Eliminate double-staffing; use 2nd staff member for roving
- Electronic SDI to faculty and students (as appropriate)
- E-mail reference
- Special information bulletin boards: in library; in departments

Increase awareness of new reference model
- Ads, flyers—in campus newspapers, on radio
- Work with advisory committees
- CWIS
- Signage—constantly revised
- Splashy PR event

User needs surveys
- Focus groups
    a) Labor intensive: requires study or experts
    b) Contract it out to reduce emotional investment in outcome
- Develop common survey instruments
    a) E.g., Duke's
    b) ACRL Performance Standards
- Transactions
  to give information about what users are actually getting at
  reference desks

Reference desk less as a physical "icon"
- Subject teams with responsibility in reference, faculty liaison, collection dev.
- More outreach
  Bring reference to department offices, dorms
- Email reference
    a) library/reference as a specific address
    b) or on a catalog menu
    c) with a workform/template as a reference interview

DUKE: SMALL GROUP TASK #2

Eliminate the traditional model of BI by empowering users and using advanced technology.
- Develop/form alliances and partnerships with vendors and campus computing centers to effect design of user friendly/standardized interfaces.
- Form alliances with educators on elementary/secondary level to promote problem-solving, critical thinking, research, analytic and advanced technological skills.

Develop greater technical expertise among reference staff
- Minimum competency requirements
- Staff development programs

Develop client centered service model
- Define what client centered means
- Identify client groups
- Develop the skills & expertise to identify client needs and expectations
- Apply skills to pilot group to identify needs and expectations

Redefine BI in terms of client-centered service
- Assess current programs in terms of client-centered needs & expectations

Staff development and BI go hand-in-hand, with a focus on the client

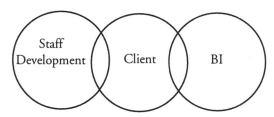

BERKELEY: SMALL GROUP TASK #2

Increase perception of reference process as a value-added service
- Document the quality
    Evaluate reference in terms of learning process and creativity
- PR in faculty newsletters
    Contributions to research and curriculum design
- Librarians involved in assignment design and curriculum planning
- Librarian liaisons to academic departments
    Faculty doctoral and freshman courses

DECISION GRID

	What constitutes?	What tools?	Who will prepare?	Who will deliver?	Where will delivery occur?
Basic Info Services					
Intermediate Info Services					
Advanced Info Services					

DUKE: SMALL GROUP TASK #2

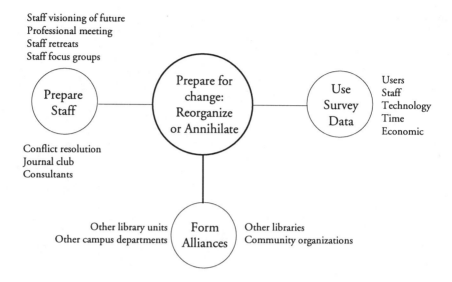

Initiate staff development for technological expertise
  • Step 1: Identify baseline skills necessary for everyone in reference
  • Identify the trainer in- or out-of-house
  • Develop the specific training program(s) and specific software and documentation
  • Implement program
  • Evaluate and return to step 1
  • Maintain point of need technical support.

Formally seek user opinion in making service decisions:
  • Focus groups
  • Log questions and analyze
  • User survey
  • Interviews

Provide better service for remote users
  • Market available services
  • Assign staff responsibility for remote access (connecting, troubleshooting, liaison)
  • Develop online help
  • E-mail reference
  • Vendor relations (represent user needs)

BERKELEY: SMALL GROUP TASK #2

Bonus outcome: Jerry Campbell's "SELECTION CRITERIA GRID"

	Cost	How long to implement?	Impact	Stand alone? or affects other units	Requires prior steps?	Etc.
Change: Develop new roles						
Promote opportunities for in-depth reference						
Meet users where they are... etc.						

DUKE: SMALL GROUP TASK #2

Change expectations
- Assess user needs and perceptions through surveys, focus groups, etc.
- Faculty outreach & liaison: "listen with big ears"; develop reference information packets (via print, electronic, and personal contact)

Advance theoretical foundations of our profession
- Study information seeking behavior
- Effective communication
- Collaborate with other disciplines, e.g. systems design

Enhance Services:
- BI Independence—develop tools responsive to local users' needs/conditions
    - use external resources (to be more efficient)
    - address different learning styles
    - curriculum-based instruction
- Maintain & expand
    - personal contact
    - consultation
    - desk

A WHAT-WHY-AND-HOW GRID

CHANGES DESIRED

	Emphasis on ACCESS for all	More effective staff development	Changes in Original & Physical Structure
Knowledge-based decision making; user analysis; market research			
Work with & influence commercial producers/vendors			
Networked pc's for every member of primary clientele			

STRATEGIES

AFTERMATH

13. MAINTAINING MOMENTUM

Anne G. Lipow

The most telling yardstick of any program whose participants are there to learn new ways of thinking about and working in their local environments is what happens afterwards. In this case, a great many participants continued contact with Institute staff and fellow participants in the weeks following each Institute, and of those, a number indicated that their own thinking had changed as a result of their Institute experience. One participant wrote, "...I think [the Institute] will be one of those watershed meetings that changes how people in a field think about things...." Another said that for him, a particular graphic displayed and discussed by one of the speakers was "like an epiphany."

However, even the most thought-provoking, highly regarded workshop of this type is a failure if its participants don't take some action based on what they learned. With this in mind, the Institute included an activity specifically designed to increase the chance that participants would transfer what they learned to what they did back home. In addition to their receiving very practical, action-specific ideas throughout the Institute—from speakers, from discussions, and from assigned tasks— participants had a chance to think about how they personally would follow-up immediately upon their return or very soon thereafter.

That chance came in the final hour of the Institute—TALKBACK. After participants gave open evaluations about what went right and what and how to improve what went awry, they were asked "How will you follow up?" Their own answers (expressed to the group or not), as well as the opportunity to hear others think out loud, constituted an important component of the next- steps planning process for each participant.

Whether or not participants would have accomplished as much follow-up as they did without some personal transformation or the groundwork to help them maintain momentum we'll never know. However, the amount and kinds of activities that have occurred in the ensuing months are, by anyone's standards, impressive. Nearly everyone we contacted had made moves to inform their colleagues about their experiences and had either held or scheduled meetings to involve fellow staff in translating at least some of those experiences to local situations.

The several ways in which participants actually followed through upon arrival home are enumerated below—for two reasons: to give readers additional perspectives on the proceedings, and to provide examples of what is possible for those wishing to encourage an aftermath of their own programs. The summaries by two participants are reproduced in their entirety in this section. Combined with the three additional summaries in journal articles by Ann Coder, Larry Oberg, and James Rettig (cited below), the reader is left with the clear impression that each participant took away something different from the Institute. The authors' unique choices of what to cover, their varied descriptions of the same event, and their distinctive interpretations testify to the complexity of the issues before us.

ARTICLES IN PUBLICATIONS

Three participants rushed summaries of their experiences to professional journals.

Ann Coder, "Rethinking Reference: New Models and How to Get There." *Hawaii Library Association Journal*, Vol. 44, June 1993, 14-16.

Larry Oberg, "Rethinking Reference: Smashing Icons at Berkeley." *C&RL News*, May 1993, 265-266.

James Rettig, "Academic Reference Service Astride a Fault Line." *Wilson Library Bulletin*, May 1993, 53-56.

LISTSERV DISCUSSIONS

Larry Oberg's summary of the proceedings on the COLLIB-L Internet discussion group immediately following the Berkeley program roused a lively exchange of ideas that was sustained for several weeks.

WRITTEN SUMMARIES FOR LOCAL COLLEAGUES

Upon returning home, several participants wrote up their experiences and distributed them to staff. Two such examples—one by Bill Whitson, the other by Ann Pettingill—appear in the next chapter, "Sharing Experiences with Colleagues."

MEETINGS WITH STAFF

Below are snippets from selected notes sent by participants describing their follow-up activities.

"[One of us] did a presentation to reference people of our local library consortium...people were excited...[Also], we're going on a library staff retreat next week and [the 3 of us participants] are planning to wear our "Rethinking" t-shirts!

"...[We participants] constituted a panel, wearing the T-shirts, at a brown bag lunch. There must have been close to 50 people who had numerous questions...There is a support group now, what a great thing for an AUL to have! This doesn't mean that all who attended the institute agree on what should be done; but ...[we] came back with definitely new ideas....[Because several from our library, not just one, attended the Institute], people now see that it is part of some mainstream thinking."

"...We decided not to wear our T-shirts to the staff meeting so as not to create a 'we-they' division...."

"I'm sure you must be hearing from others who have attempted to replicate the rethinking workshop in their organizations. I've just completed the process with my group...over a period of three mornings, and I and my staff were very pleased..."

"[We] are putting together a meeting to kick off several more meetings to discuss [our library's] information services model of the future, and we [plan to include] several of the Institute handouts in our program..."

"Just wanted you to know that...I've really been trying to apply at least some of what I learned at the Duke Institute here at home. I conducted our last two reference staff meetings by the consensus method, and the librarians thought that it was really a useful way to do things. I facilitated the first one, in which we identified issues we needed to discuss and prioritized them. Another staff member facilitated the second one, in which we discussed the top priority issue and ... some subissues and came to consensus on some approaches. I was chided in the second meeting for talking too much by one [colleague]—so I guess that's a sign of success (of sorts)."

"All staff interested in reference services are invited to attend a panel presentation and discussion on "New Directions for Reference Services"...Several librarians who attended the recent "Rethinking Reference" Institute will report on what they learned...and propose ways in which some of the new directions identified in the workshop might be applied here...." *From announcement in library staff newsletter*

DISCUSSIONS AT ALA

At the June 1993 Annual Conference of the American Library Association, the Reference and Adult Services Division set aside time at its program meeting for a report about the Institutes. Also, a few Institute participants organized an ad hoc meeting at the Conference to inform others and continue discussions.

14 • SHARING EXPERIENCES WITH COLLEAGUES

This chapter contains the written impressions of the Institute by participants Bill Whitson, University of California, Berkeley, then a reference librarian, now Service Innovation Coordinator in Research Services, and Ann Pettingill, Head of Reference at Old Dominion University in Chesapeake, Virginia. The papers represent their thinking of the moment: a response to what happened immediately before, with a considerable sense of urgency to produce the papers within a very short time afterwards. They are therefore not to be judged as the deliberated product that would be expected of published material. • *Editor*

BILL WHITSON'S SUMMARY

March 23, 1993

To: Reference Colleagues
From: Bill Whitson
Re: Rethinking Reference: Report

Here is what I think I learned.

1.   What is reference service?

Helping people get "unstuck."

As people set out to find information resources that will help them solve a problem or work out a process of creative thought, they get "stuck" at various points along the way. The problem may be major—not knowing where to begin—or minor—what does this abbreviation mean?—and in most cases, the information seeker CAN eventually get unstuck without our help, either by puzzling over it long enough, by finding and reading instructions or explanations, by asking someone else, by trial and error, or by simply ignoring the problem and going around it. With reference service, people find better information, faster and more easily.

Reference service consists of two elements:
(1) expertise and (2) availability.

Expertise means knowledge of resources and of the process of finding information, and the interpersonal skills that enable us to understand what an information seeker really "needs" in order to get unstuck. Both are a matter of degree and each reference service provider will offer a unique combination. The more one knows, the more intelligent one is, the more sensitive and insightful one is, the more articulate, etc., the better. It increases the probability one will be helpful in any given reference encounter. "True" reference questions (i.e., those involving retrieval of information or knowledge useful to a person's thought process) do not have "right" answers. It is always a matter of judgment, and to a considerable extent, a function of the amount of time available for the exchange.

Availability means being there when the person gets stuck, and for long enough to help effectively. One can be available by being physically present, or by being reachable by phone, e-mail, or other means. Availability is usually also a matter of degree: how easy it is to establish contact and how quickly a response may be obtained. Someone studying in a library may simply walk across a room. Another may have to travel from home to a service point in a library during certain hours, entailing considerable effort, time and a long "wait" (interval between when the question arose and when the answer can be obtained). Another may write a letter, leave a phone message or send an e-mail, and receive a reply after some period of time.

Obviously, for the person with the question, the easier it is to establish contact, and the quicker the response, the better. For the library, it is mostly a matter of cost. Since we provide the service free, we are always required to "ration" the availability of the service in some fashion. Obviously, we should try to be as responsive as possible to user needs, given the budget available.

2. Why do we need to rethink reference?

We have always had to be "rethinking" reference, since we have always had to ration service. There is nothing here that is really new.

The problem is simply **increasing demand** (or **need**) and **shrinking resources.** (If we had adequate resources, we would naturally and easily adapt to the changes brought about by technology. In other words, technology is a red herring in this context.)

3. How can we deal with this problem?

We have **three** options:

1. Decrease service.

This means further rationing either the level of expertise or its availability.

Shorter hours. Fewer service points. Less telephone or e-mail access. Fewer staff with less time to give each question. Less expert staff.

2. Change priorities.

We can rethink which services we provide, or the relative support we give to each one. This should ideally involve user studies to be sure we are making the best choices.

Examples: Increase or decrease "desk hours" or expertise of those at the desk. Increase user education (handouts, tutorials,

111

classes) as compensation for lack of reference service. Cut back user education efforts as less "cost-effective" in order to devote resources to reference service. Increase or decrease reference by appointment—the in-depth research consultation. Increase or decrease use of phone, e-mail, etc.

3. Work smarter and harder.

We can look carefully at every detail of our operation and see how it might be done in a more "cost-effective" way.

This is the heart of the matter. There is a general perception that most reference departments have not worked hard enough at this—that we waste resources by clinging to outmoded or unnecessary traditional practices. We need a healthy dose of systems analysis, the imaginative use of all forms of technology (from signs to expert systems), and careful redesigning of jobs, to insure that whatever can be done by lower-paid staff is reassigned appropriately.

This always raises the knotty issue of whether expertise is being appropriately compensated. Since more expertise always enables one to provide better service, the Library tends to always take full advantage of whatever expertise level the staff member brings to the role. Whenever the staff member has a higher level of expertise than is recognized in his/her employment classification, one could argue that that employee is being "exploited." Conversely, if a highly paid staff member is dealing much of the time with questions which do not appear to require much expertise, he or she may be viewed as "underutilized."

One aspect of this problem is the issue of the M.L.S., or of classification in the librarian series. To what extent do these correlate with expertise, or protect employees from being "exploited"? I personally believe there is some correlation, and that the long effort to establish librarianship as a "profession" has had a measurable impact on giving librarians a fairer level of status and compensation than they would have had otherwise.

In practice, however, we cannot afford to rely entirely on persons classified as librarians when it comes to providing reference service. Therefore, our only course is to (1) select reference staff carefully, to make sure they have the potential to function at the required level of expertise; (2) train reference staff adequately, and provide ample opportunities for continuing education; (3) structure job roles, and reference staffing patterns, to minimize the extent to which staff are called upon to deal with matters beyond their expertise level, and (4) classify reference staff at high enough levels to insure appropriate compensation and recognition.

NOTES BY ANN PETTINGILL

I wrote up these notes upon my return from Duke after the Rethinking Reference Conference for each of the reference librarians and for my director and AUL, with appropriate handouts. The reference department will be using the notes and articles as a point of departure in a series of meetings we will be holding for the rest of the summer on changes in reference services and priorities, and on the development of new services. —A.P.

June 4, 1993

1. Jerry Campbell, Duke Director of Library and Academic Computing: "In Search of New Foundations." This talk was based largely on his article, "Shaking the Conceptual Foundations of Reference: A Perspective."

    A. Need to develop conceptual clarity on the role of reference librarians— need a clear sense of mission to define new roles effectively. This is necessary for providing a benchmark for gauging progress and also for providing a common ground for discussion

    B. Need for data re the practice of reference. At Duke they began this spring to try and diagram reference work:

    > Track reference questions over a period of time
    > Causes of reference questions? e.g.,
    >> environment
    >> library methods
    >> people
    >> equipment usage or problems
    >> procedures
    >> technology

C. Then, look at the reasons for questions. Are there systemic reasons (e.g., confusing building problems) which could be remedied in order to eliminate certain confusing situations which tend to cause questions? Chart out the causes to see if you can perceive patterns in the questions (this is based on TQM Pareto Charts).

D. Need consumer analysis. What does consumer need? want? Right now, we (meaning librarians in general) serve up information on our own terms and expect users to meet those terms—this is not just a reference problem. We limit user responses by the choices we allow; we really do not know how they want information.

At Duke currently: they wrote an outline describing where they want to be in the year 2010; where they are now; steps for the move from here to there. They then hired a survey firm to undertake a study of users' perception of changes, library services now and in the future, etc. The firm held focus groups for faculty, grad, undergrad, staff in order to air problems, ideas, and to build information to be included in an extensive 4-part survey. This survey has been completed and carried out; they expect that the initial analysis will be complete by July 2. The focus groups brought out such requests as the desire for databases which are easily accessible, fast, labor saving, free, computerized, networked, comprehensive; need people to assist in use and interpretation.

June 5, 1993

2. Terry Mazany, Consultant. Terry is a consultant on organizational change who frequently works with school systems, government, and nonprofit organizations in effecting change; he acts as a negotiator to assist in the process; he has worked with library systems also.

He emphasized that, when you are working in a group to come up with a common vision or to discuss changes, it is very important to set ground rules by which all participants agree to act. They can govern whatever the participants wish, such as times for discussions, appropriate behavior for participants, etc. The ground rules set for this particular group of 60 participants in a medium-sized room were:

- talk in small voices; listen with big ears (to facilitate small group discussions throughout the room)

114

- allow and continuously monitor equal time for each person to talk in small group discussions
- quickly conclude conversation when asked to focus back on the large group
- identify a facilitator, recorder, presenter, and process observer

This is also a model for group process.

What do we know about the process of change? What type of leadership is appropriate for change? How do we design involvement and continuous improvement into the change process? For change to be effective, we need both process AND content.

Terry pointed out a study by Weisberg(?) concerning how corporations approached the process of evaluation and change over the last 100 or so years.

Early 1900's: the experts solved the problems
1950's: everybody solved the problems
1965: experts improve whole systems
1990's: everybody improves whole systems

Gradually more and more people have been involved in the process. What is a strategic planning model for change?

1. where are we?
2. where do we want to go?
3. how do we get there?
4. how do we know we got there?

From his observations of hundreds of change processes, Terry has put together a model of what happens during an effective change process:

Phase I Awareness	Phase II Agreement

Phase III Research

Phase IV Consensus

Phase V Implement	Phase VI Improve

The Change Process:

Phase I.
    Awareness and taking stock; creating the vision cannot take
    place until participants have gone through a period of learning
    and readiness; also, a new vision of service cannot be created
    without the addition of new knowledge.
        survey of issues
        analysis of performance
        build problem-solving capacity
        identify short term success factors
        construct short term action plans

Phase II. Agreements
        consensus building capacity
        set up structures for involvement
        innovative practices
        identify service outcomes
        identify essential conditions
        construct a preliminary vision
        conflict resolution
        set the criteria for the improvement model

Phase III. Inquiry and research
        site visits
        literature study
        study groups
        data collection
        establish baseline measures
        identify innovative strategies
        experimentation

Phase IV. Library-wide consensus and commitment
        advanced vision constructed
        library redesign project plan
        achieve authentic consensus

Phase V. Implementation
        identification of success factors
        project monitoring
        process assessment

Phase VI. Reflection and continuous improvement
evaluation of service outcomes
project planning

What group processes facilitate the process of coming to a consensus?
listening
compromising
incorporating new ideas
inviting participation
having a common purpose that you have agreed to
time for consideration
flexibility
trust among members
brainstorming   time
preparation   trust
clear goals   leadership
non-threatening, tolerant environment

Leadership. Most organizations start as autocratic. We do not have many models from any part of life for a non-autocratic organization. We have little practice with alternatives. In moving from autocracy, organizations will usually go in one of two ways: democracy, where everyone votes; or laissez-faire, where anything goes. Often these two models lead to a lack of direction and a feeling of purposelessness. We need a new vision of leadership—participatory, synergistic, facilitative. This is a **key shift**. Leadership gradually becomes a function rather than a position.

What to look for? These things are typical of consensus:
lack of disagreement
"I can live with that"
thinking or feeling together
respect for everyone in the group
everyone buys in to some degree
willingness to go along
lack of clearly defined opposition
a vote is not taken
everyone participates

Information from the Rand Change Agent Study on the nature of organizational change:

- Change is a problem of the smallest unit—the people on the front line; it is that the determination is made as to how and whether ideas are implemented
- Policy cannot mandate change
- Local variability is the rule; plan for it
- Initial motivation is not crucial; belief can follow behavior
- Outside consultants can help, but they must interact with, and adjust effectively, to the local setting
- Projects narrowly aimed at discrete aspects of the system are likely to fail—bold, comprehensive projects are more likely to produce greater change
- content and process of change both matter
- Networking among staff is an effective mechanism for achieving change
- Removing constraints does not ensure effective practice
- Project resources do not predict outcomes
- Implementation finally determines outcomes

The issue of power. Power = authority + influence. The autocratic model pits authority vs. influence. Consensus is a vehicle to unite the two.

When two groups are on the opposing sides of an issue, the best way to start reaching consensus is **not** putting each "position" out on the table (the way you would do in labor negotiations, for instance). It is much more workable to start with "interests," why the position is important to you. For instance, Terry worked with the Detroit school system on the issue of uniforms for students. Parents said "yes" and students said "no way." Terry got them to take their **positions** off the table and start with their **interests**; parents said that cost of designer clothes was a big issue for them, and safety of the students was another. Students said that self-esteem from nice clothes was important to them, and the principle of individual freedom was another. They heard each others' concerns and then worked together to come up with new ideas to resolve the difference. They came up with a 3-part solution: 1. certain items were off-limits at all times: gold jewelry; designer shoes; leather jackets. 2. everyone agreed on a range of clothing types which were okay to wear. 3. Fridays were declared free days—with the exception of the #1 items, students could be really creative and wear what they wanted every Friday. This solution made everyone involved feel very positive because it incorporated the issues that each group considered important.

Decision making types

1. Command. A decision is made and will be implemented
2. Consultation. What are your thoughts on this issue before I have to make a decision?
3. Collaboration. Leader sets up parameters ahead and then abides by consensus.
4. Consensus. Group takes the responsibility for the decision.

Problem: can a committee be held responsible for its decision? This is a big paradigm shift for our society. Terry used an interesting example of a big change in mythology for our modern (US) society: the move from Superman, one individual with huge powers taking care of all problems to Teenage Mutant Ninja Turtles, a group of 4 individuals with equal responsibilities, with a coach off to the side. He says that the committee can share in responsibility and accountability if we begin to perceive it on those terms. The group holds itself to be responsible, and it shares in a process of continuous improvement.

In consensus forming, empowerment is essential. All stakeholders on an issue must be represented in the discussion and decision making. Don't set up a committee that does not have the authority for the decision embedded in it. Always ask, "is the solution better than doing nothing?" Or is it worse than doing nothing? Asking these questions is a good way to avoid watering down the decision to such a low common denominator that it is meaningless (common in a democratic process).

I have more information from Terry Mazany. If anyone is interested, let me know and I will lend you his document.

3. Suzanne Calpestri, Head, Cooperative Services Department, UC Berkeley

   There are many conditions currently forcing changes in library and reference services:

   > budget reductions
   > increasing and changing user needs
   > information explosion
   > rapidly changing technology
   > expanded job assignments

   The most frequent set of responses by libraries to problems of this nature in the past seems to be:

   > looking inward to solve problems
   > trying to do it all
   > working faster to do it all
   > excluding certain groups
   > withdrawing either formally or de facto from agreements
   > insulate
   > shift responsibility

   These responses do not solve problems. We need new approaches:

   > look outward
   >> restructure or create new alliances
   >> change our focus
   >> compete to stimulate growth
   >> take collective responsibility

4. Virginia Massey-Burzio, Head of Resources, Johns Hopkins U, formerly Head of Reference at Brandeis.

   She led the process at Brandeis that ended in the elimination of the reference desk, establishment of an information desk and a consultative service by librarians. She did the same thing at Hopkins, only it was much easier there—everyone was more prepared for change. The information desk is mainly directional and questions are 1-2 minutes. Grad students and paraprofessionals screen and make referrals. The research consultation service: BI, collection development, consultation, orientation to new students, serves one individual at a time. Previous system of reference desk overemphasized user accessibility to librarian and meant that there was not enough time to devote to substantive questions.

5. Frances Painter, Director of Administrative Services,
Va. Tech Libraries.

Tech has been reexamining its mission and organization to emphasize
access to services. They have action plans each year for librarians.
They have emphasized staff training and tried to incorporate things
like workshops on managing stress and change; they recognize the
need for reference staff to learn new products, etc. and support this
with a policy of assistance from other departments. They have eliminated the AUL levels. Organizational responsibilities have moved
downward and outward. Part of the decision-making process is constant questioning and evaluating—much more than before. Also many
processes never discussed before have been brought out into the open;
everyone has much more information for real decision making. They
are trying to build flexibility into staff position descriptions, create
systems to recognize achievements, and establish job rotation within
libraries.

6. Janice Simmons-Wellburn, Head of Main Library Reference,
U of Iowa.

They have a program called Library Navigator and are developing
another—Library Explorer, search tactics for the new student. They
have set up a multi-media information arcade in the main library.
New name: Information and Instructional Services. They are moving
away from the idea that reference is a physical location with on-
demand provision, more networked processes; focussing on instruction and outreach; have reduced cataloging.

7. Larry Oberg, University Librarian at Willamette University.

Spoke on paraprofessionals—need to rethink their responsibilities
and involve them in this process.

8. Group discussions and recommendations.

Seven groups met throughout Saturday and Sunday to experience the
consensus-making process and to come up with ideas on how libraries
will change in the future. We used five overall areas: Organizational
Structure; Staffing; Tools and Equipment; Services; Clients. These
are attached with the descriptions from all the groups. The second

121

part is a list of services that should or will be reduced or cut from libraries in order to begin doing all the things in Part 1. There was a lot of discussion on all aspects of user instruction. The following is an expansion of recommendations from all the groups describing ideas on "small victories"—concrete actions to effect change and move towards the new services and functions described in the five overall areas from Part 1. Each group chose several themes and suggested specific changes or actions for those areas. I copied these down as they were read off by each group leader:

Prepare staff for change
>   set up a journal club (group reading same articles and discussing them)
>   staff computer bulletin board
>   conflict resolution
>   staff focus groups
>   professional meetings (or bring speakers in)
>   consultant

Form alliances
>   other libraries
>   other departments within libraries
>   campus departments
>   community organizations

Advance the theoretical foundations of the profession
>   study information-seeking behavior
>   effective communication
>   collaborate with other disciplines—e.g., systems design

Enhance services
>   BI independence
>   develop tools responsive to local users' needs/conditions
>   use external resources—rely on what others have developed
>   address different learning styles
>   curriculum based instruction—partnership with faculty
>   maintain and expand personal contact
>   free librarians time for higher-level tasks
>   assess use of ref. desk: how many staff, what level, etc.
>   simplify processes

eliminate duplication
conduct workload studies

Develop a client-center service model
define what client-centered means
identify client groups
develop skills and expertise to identify clients' needs and
expectations
apply skills to pilot group

Change organizational structure and relationships
abolish the AUL level of administration
close down the reference desk for one week and spend the
time trying out alternative methods

Formally seek user opinions
focus groups
log questions and answers
user surveys
interviews

Better services for remote users
market available services more effectively
assign specific responsibility for troubleshooting connec-
tivity problems
develop on-line assistance methods
e-mail reference
investigate vendor relations—represent user needs for improved products

Ongoing staff development at all levels
go back to the library and share the results of "Rethinking
Reference Institute"
during meetings, at least one person has to report on new
technology
each person in the group/dept/etc. suggests and gets group
agreement on what item they will drop, reallocate
to another level, etc.
free up staff time for "playing"
reach consensus on these changes

Staff development for technical expertise

    identify baseline skills for all in reference

    identify a trainer (in-house or outside)

    identify specific training programs, documentation, and
        software

    implement

    evaluate and return to step one

15 • THE FUTURE OF BIBLIOGRAPHIC INSTRUCTION: AN UNRESOLVED ISSUE

RETHINKING INFORMATION ACCESS

A RESPONSE TO "RETHINKING INFORMATION ACCESS"

TO BI OR NOT TO BI? THAT IS THE QUESTION

Nothing on or off the agenda inspired such spirited exchange at the Duke Institute as the question "In the new reference model, will bibliographic instruction services increase or decrease?" No consensus could be reached at either Institute, but at Berkeley the views along the full spectrum of possibilities were expressed and left at that, whereas at Duke, the discussion took on the semblance of a debate. Noticing participants' frustration that there was insufficient time at the Institute to develop their ideas more fully, the organizers invited particular proponents to submit their views in writing, to be published in these *Proceedings*. Thus the three papers in this chapter. Again, the reader is reminded, as in the case of the participants' summaries in the previous chapter, these papers represent views-in-progress and are therefore not to be judged as the well-worked-out product that would normally be expected of published material. • *Editor*

RETHINKING INFORMATION ACCESS

Kenneth W. Berger, Johannah Sherrer and Rich Hines

Perkins Library Reference Department
Duke University, Durham, North Carolina

June 1993

INTRODUCTION

Rethinking Reference (East) gave attendees many opportunities to hear about and discuss new ways to look at organizational structure, staffing of reference operations, and allocation of professional and support staff in accomplishing the varied tasks of reference departments. For some of those in attendance, however, there are more basic questions that have less to do with library staff than with present and emerging technologies. At one general session this issue was discussed, though the lively interchange was too quickly sidetracked into a debate on the future (if any) of library user instruction programs as technologies. Lest the substance of the debate on the importance and potential impact of developing technologies be underrepresented in the published proceedings of the institute, Anne Lipow challenged attendees to prepare essays which represent different points of view expressed at that forum.

The introduction of automated technologies—in this case referring to the many uses and forms of computerization and electronic communications—has long had recognized effects on library operations and use. None of us can deny that these technologies have made it possible to increase our efficiency, offer new services to users, and in many ways facilitate the use of libraries by our patrons. At the same time, two situations, one internal and one external to our buildings and profession, exist which have serious implications for the future of the library as an institution, and specifically for the role and mission of the reference librarian. First, too often we have used the new technologies to merely transfer traditional library structure, organization and access to computerized formats, without removing the barriers to information-seeking independence that keep our users dependent upon us. Second, there has developed outside the library institution an entirely new world of information access that is directed to independent use by present and potential library users.

As stated above, the debate at the Institute soon centered around library user instruction programs. There was some quibbling over what to call these activities (e.g., bibliographic instruction), but the crux of the matter was why we have them now, and whether we would still need them in the future. Library user instruction is not the sole focus of the debate over the impact of new technologies in libraries, but it is a useful illustration of the problems inherent in the first of the two situations described above.

END USER INDEPENDENCE?

Why do we institute BI programs? There have been two primary reasons. One, though not necessarily the most important, was to introduce users to people who work in the library (i.e., reference librarians) who would be available to assist them in fulfilling their information needs. Another, and for many a more significant reason, is to teach library research skills, ranging from the most basic (e.g., how to look up the call number of a book) to the most sophisticated. Another aspect of the broader concept of BI is the provision of user guides (handouts, signs, instructional programs, etc.).

Why do we have to teach these skills? Obviously, now more than ever, the world of publication, and, more broadly, the world of information, is extremely complex and varied. There is no single standard for either production or access to these materials, and no simple map to find and use them. Hence we have libraries. But in the attempt to collect and organize this treasure trove, the library institution itself is a mass of confusion—even to those members of its profession.

If our sole purpose was to be the masters of the treasure, we could serve to directly answer each and every user question, to provide every bit of information or published item the user might want without the user having to do anymore than make a clear request (the clarity being reached, of course, with our professional assistance). Even if these were our goals, it is physically and fiscally impossible. Furthermore, our users do not want to be so dependent upon us—most, at some level, want to be confident and capable enough to retrieve what they need on their own, when they want to do it. (This feeling certainly carries into most other aspects of our lives. If we had to get assistance every time we went into a store, we would be more likely to go to a competing—and less expensive!—establishment which allows us to search the shelves on our own.) Hence, we lead tours, we hold classes, and we produce guides to make users more independent.

We go further than that. We do try to make the library easier to use. We replaced card catalogs with online catalogs. We replaced printed indexes with computerized indexes. (Yes, both card catalogs and printed indexes do often co-exist with their electronic counterparts in many of our institutions, but which ones do our users most often use? Which ones do we most often use?) We look at our sign systems and redesign building layouts. All to remove more barriers to successful, independent use by non-professionals.

If we were to carry these instructional and service activities to the extreme, we would eventually create a library that is completely self-evident, so any user could navigate the world of information and retrieve what he or she desired. Obviously this is an ideal, but isn't it what we should be working towards? The alternative, after all, is to imply we would always maintain barriers to user independence in order to perpetuate the need for reference librarians.

IN SEARCH OF A NEW MODEL

So where is the model for how we make these giant leaps? So far, at least, it hasn't shown up in the library community. We continue to struggle with BI programs, and we have yet to prove they are very effective. If we see them eliminating many basic questions and enabling our users to come to us with more sophisticated requests, that only raises the level of the kind of help they need from us. (Or perhaps it just hastens the need, for shouldn't we have assumed all along that they always needed the answers to those questions as well, but that it just took too long to get to that level?)

We continue to produce library point-of-use materials, struggling to find the right mix of information that will meet the most needs. In the process we continue to leave each individual user, with his or her individual needs, lost in a mass of irrelevancies as each searches for the information that is specifically needed.

We continue to put out more and more computer stations, amazed at the information that users have at their fingertips. Having little faith in the user's ability to navigate through the CD-ROMs and networked (i.e., the Internet) resources, we continue to offer tours, classes, handouts and in-person assistance. And well we should, for too many of these options have structures designed by librarians, or at least for librarians or library users (i.e., those who have developed certain minimal library use skills).

129

The answer lies not in the world of libraries, but in the world of consumers. In front of us are two computer software and hardware products catalogues. One is from Power Up!®, and the other from TigerSoftware®. Each includes CD-ROM players and, between them, dozens of CD-ROM products, many of them what we would call reference tools. The market targeted for these catalogs is not libraries! The market is the family with its own personal computer. And it is a tremendous market indeed. Shouldn't reference librarians be asking themselves why people are shelling out significant funds to buy these products when the information is free from their library? Shouldn't reference librarians be asking themselves why people are able to be successful and comfortable enough in their use of the products to maintain such impressive market growth?

Millions of individuals (not just companies and libraries) have accounts on the major online services, especially CompuServe®, America Online® and Prodigy®. Although many kinds of resources are available from these services, most of their offerings are of information. People spend an average of $100 a year to subscribe, not including the costs of the computer equipment, modems and extra searching charges. (This user population includes a member of our support staff—not a highly paid group of workers—who is a single mother who subscribes for her school-age daughter!) Shouldn't reference librarians be asking themselves why people are shelling out significant funds to buy these products when the information is free from their library? Shouldn't reference librarians be asking themselves why people are able to be successful and comfortable enough in their use of the products to maintain such impressive market growth?

There have been numerous reports in the news media lately about impending developments in cable television access to hundreds more channels than are currently available. Many of the new offerings will be informational, even interactive, and they are all directed at the end user. Shouldn't reference librarians be asking themselves why people are shelling out significant funds to buy these products when the information is free from their library? Shouldn't reference librarians be asking themselves why people are able to be successful and comfortable enough in their use of the products to maintain such impressive market growth?

The simple fact is that the business community is demonstrating an information-seeking and retrieval model which is increasingly by-passing the library institution. Yes, there are computer services and software companies that maintain help staff, usually available via phone, but for the online services in particular the emphasis is on designing systems that the average user can manipulate—independently. Even though services like CompuServe and America Online offer online, interactive help, the point is that they don't have to have people you can meet with face to face, they don't have to have instruction classes, and they don't have to have reams of printed instructional materials. Time is money for both these companies and their subscribers; a system that wasn't designed "user friendly" would not be financially viable for either.

These services have another thing in common in terms of a model for reference services: they are both responsive to the needs of users. At the Rethinking Reference Institute we heard repeated use of the term "client centered." If these online services were not client centered in the design and content of their product, they could not exist.

The point is that much of what we do for the user is based on the premise that either users need to know how information is organized (i.e., produced, distributed, indexed, accessed and obtained), or—and assuming that most users lack this knowledge—they must turn to professionals (i.e., reference librarians) to assist them in their information seeking activities. Underlying the work of reference librarians is the structure of the library, serviced in large part by the support staff which do most of the library-end activities in the organization-of-knowledge process—and may even participate in the process of directly assisting end users. Technology (in this case referring to everything from typewriters to computers) has served more to assist the library staff than end users, as the former continue to serve as intermediaries for the latter. The concept is qualitatively, if not quantitatively, illustrated in Figure 1. Note that the same graphic could illustrate the traditional situation in other professions such as medicine and law.

In Figure 2 the influence of technological advances exhibits significant impact of personnel involvement at both ends. (Again, consider that the new structure applies equally to other professions.) Support staff are not as involved in processing materials as more publications and information sources are available through centralized, networked systems. Their role in direct patron interaction is also reduced as these systems become more designed for end user manipulation. Similarly, professionals are now performing fewer tasks, as they concentrate on high-end activities such as system design and assisting end users when higher level information-access expertise is required.

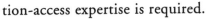

FIGURE 1

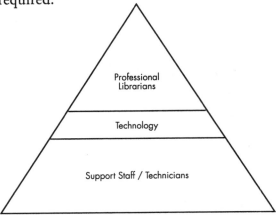

Where technology has little impact, end users are dependent upon professional assistance in identifying and obtaining information (or in training to do so), and in support staff operations for the activities which make the materials available.

FIGURE 2

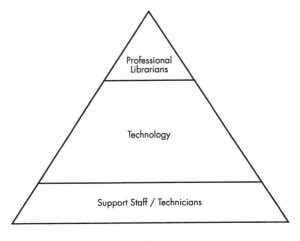

As the impact of technology on information access increases, and end user searching and retrieval becomes faster, easier and more effective, the need for professional and non-professional assistance decreases.

With this increasing availability of end-user systems, and with the explosion of text and reference resources becoming available independent of library institutions, the role of reference librarians must change. The first step in dealing with the new information environment is to recognize that it is happening. Denial will not make it go away.

Next, there are some strategies that can be useful as we assist our users in the transition to the future. For example:

1. In the past librarians have been very good at mastering published information resources, and even computerized resources, as they are aimed at the library market; we need to become equally expert at other, non-traditional and emerging resources which are being used in the business community and by independently directed information seekers.

2. We must concentrate on acquiring electronic access technology which is designed for non-librarian end users, rather than for librarian intermediaries, and we must communicate this strategy to database and other electronic information producers and publishers.

3. As we endeavor to make the systems we provide more user friendly, develop collaborative efforts with the commercial organizations which have successfully met the challenges of creating effective end user interfaces.

4. We need to negotiate campus-wide access to their services, at rates attractive to our institutions and users, and in volume attractive to the commercial firms.

5. We need to negotiate with commercial and academic publishers to get online access to their products, paying on a per-use basis; the data is probably on disk anyway, and publishers would be able to cut their production and distribution costs.

6. We must look at reference service as an option that will appeal to an increasingly self-sufficient user population; this means we will have to be more technically able and more willing to deal with a changing mix of user groups with more personalized service.

Finally, read media reports on what is happening, check catalogs to see what people are buying—in short, become more aware of the changing world around us. Be flexible, be open, be daring, be brave. And most of all, keep that user-centered focus that has always marked our profession, as we continually strive to make important information-related user tasks ever easier and more efficient.

A RESPONSE TO
"RETHINKING INFORMATION ACCESS"

Karen Williams
University of Arizona Library
Tucson, Arizona

A cademic librarianship as a profession has come to a crossroads. We are facing fundamental changes, many of which are the direct result of technological advances. There are other contributing factors including reduced funding for higher education and a call for more accountability from our constituents. If we are to remain viable as a profession, we must be prepared to respond to these changes, and to recognize that this response will cause us to examine our philosophies, our structure, and our activities and services. I believe that this must happen in all areas of librarianship, but the area that caused the most lively debate at the recent Rethinking Reference (East) conference was the future of bibliographic instruction.

Berger, Sherrer and Hines acknowledge this need for role change in their arguments than we must use technology more effectively, and to do work differently than we have always done in the past. Although not so explicitly stated in this paper, their conclusion during the conference debate was that if we use technology to its fullest, there will be no need for user instruction in the future. While I agree with their supporting arguments, and even with the strategies which close this piece, I think the authors have built upon an incomplete premise regarding both the terminology associated with, and the purpose of our instructional efforts and therefore, have drawn the wrong conclusions.

WHAT'S IN A NAME?

Little significance is attached to the debate over terminology, when, in essence, this debate reflects the evolutionary nature of the activity itself. The way we describe our educational efforts determines the way we think about them, and ultimately how we carry them out. We first called this activity Library Orientation, then Library Instruction, and now Bibliographic Instruction. Our primary objectives have changed from physical orientation, to a focus on local collections and services, to teaching of bibliographic structure and evaluation of materials. A dozen or so years ago when the Bibliographic Instruction Section (BIS) of ACRL and the Library Instruction Round Table were forming in ALA, these terms may have been adequate to describe the task at hand. While these terms may still be used to describe an individual activity, they are inadequate as an overarching concept. Remote access and document delivery systems lessen (or eliminate) the need to be familiar with a particular library building, or even with local collections. BIS has recently appointed a task force called "What's In a Name," to poll the membership and explore the renaming of the section. This is more than just a matter of semantics. It reflects the willingness of the profession to accept new roles and activities. It is not my intent to champion a bold new term in this response, but rather to focus on the idea that there will be a tremendous need for user education in the future, but the activities associated with this concept will change in response to a changing environment. Our primary role will not end with introducing users to the library and the people who work there, or with teaching bibliographic retrieval techniques. It will not end with providing well-designed facilities, good signage, and user-friendly software programs. These activities will continue—many of them in an automated format that does not require an intermediary. We do want to make patrons as self sufficient as possible, if for no other reason than the fact that most of our clientele will graduate and leave the institution. They need to learn how to be continuous learners. But the activities mentioned above are part of a larger goal for user education.

NEW DIRECTIONS

Let's say for the sake of argument that we can remove all barriers to retrieving needed information. Does this eliminate the need for education? Absolutely not! It simply allows us to shift our focus to those high-end activities described by the authors. Whether or not we should have been doing this all along is a moot point, but irrelevant to our discussion of how we envision the future.

To say that the need for user education will be eliminated assumes that our patrons always recognize when they need more information, can translate that need into a question that can be plugged into an information network, understand enough about the structure of information to know where to plug that query in, can evaluate the results of their search retrieval, and can manage the growing amount of available information for their own purposes. The value of a cleverly designed, end user focused cd-rom database for newspaper articles is lost when the user is unaware of newspaper articles as a source of very current information, or tries to search this database for journal articles or books.

The phrase most commonly used in the literature to describe this shift in focus is information literacy. An information-literate populace understands the importance in a democratic society of such information policy issues as copyright and the privatization of government information. They can evaluate not only individual sources, but the reliability and effectiveness of various information channels such as libraries and commercial vendors. CompuServe and Prodigy will not be able to meet all user needs any more than an individual library can.

It is important to note that technology is a tool, not a value, a goal, or an end in itself. If we use this tool to provide basic instruction and to create systems that do not require a human intermediary, we will be able to focus more creative energy on how to bring information policy issues to the attention of the campus, and how to integrate the values inherent in information literacy into the core curriculum. We will need to form new partnerships with faculty, campus teaching centers, and curriculum advisory bodies. Viewed in this way, the concept of information literacy becomes our goal, while library orientation and bibliographic instruction are methods of achieving this goal. Our focus is on the user, not the collections. We will continue to develop collections as one way of meeting user needs, but will think much more broadly than what we can own locally. And with this, I support the strategies with which Berger, Sherrer, and Hines have closed their piece, and share their commitment to building a user-centered organization. This is an exciting time to be a librarian.

TO BI OR NOT TO BI?
THAT IS THE QUESTION

James Rettig

Assistant University Librarian for Reference and Information Services
College of William and Mary, Williamsburg, Virginia

At both the Berkeley and the Duke "Rethinking Reference" Institutes, there was a decided lack of consensus on whether academic reference service of the future will feature more bibliographic instruction or less bibliographic instruction. On the surface there were two polarly opposed positions; in reality this participant in both institutes believes that there were a multitude of positions. Time did not permit the participants to articulate the nuances of their individual positions on this issue; nor was there time enough to build consensus. About the only thing all seemed to agree on was that general-purpose guided tours of library facilities would become a thing of the past. The reasons for agreeing to this varied, however. Some were willing to discontinue this service because they believe staff are too pressured to continue it; others have concluded that tours have no significant benefit for those who take them; and others were opposed to them because they are rarely conducted at "the teachable moment." "To BI or not to BI" is a major unresolved question about the shape and characteristics of the reference service of the future. This question deserves fuller exploration. The three pieces in this "Aftermath" section can promote that discussion in the field at large and by the participants in the CIC institutions' Institute to be held in Iowa in late February of 1994.

A RANGE OF REASONS

The apparent polarity of positions on BI stems from a range of reasons. One is semantic. Some dislike the term "bibliographic instruction" and would like to find a new term for a new concept. Others mean different things when they speak of "bibliographic instruction." For some it means a comprehensive program of instruction designed to make library users independent, critically thinking, lifelong learners. For others it means considerably less and is always very need-specific—for example, teaching a student how to read the entries in an index that the reference librarian has helped that student select in order to find information on a particular topic for a given assignment.

It was never clear, furthermore, whether participants were thinking about group instruction in anticipation of needs or individualized instruction at the time of need or some combination of both. The reference models discussed at the Institutes—research consultation service, reference roving, etc.—emphasize individual interactions, not group approaches. So, one could hypothesize that group sentiment at the Institutes was less kindly disposed towards group instruction than to individualized instruction, less kindly disposed towards anticipatory instruction than to time-of-need instruction; however the evidence in support of this hypothesis is at best circumstantial. Yet it is a distinction that needs to be explored.

Another reason for the apparent polarity is the lack of definition of a time frame for the "future." Some participants may have been taking a considerably longer view than others. Those whose view extended deep into the future tended, it seemed, to place a much lower value on instruction. These participants tended to place responsibility on system designers (of both electronic systems and of other systems such as reference service points in a library) to design them in such a way that users can use them without instruction. One participant in the Duke Institute described this as "nirvana" and reminded his colleagues that we have to get through the here-and-now and the short-term future before we reach nirvana—if, indeed, we ever reach it. What was not clear was how to reach it nor how long it will or ought to take to do so.

Yet another reason for the apparent polarity of positions may lie in values. Values questions were most explicitly introduced into the Berkeley Institute by participant Charles Bunge's cogent questions and comments. As a member of the Duke Institute's faculty, Professor Bunge had additional opportunities to raise such questions and to infuse the broader discussion with considerations of our values and their practical, programmatic implications. It may simply be that instruction is a deeply held value for some academic librarians but not for others. Indeed, participants in some of the small group discussions at both Institutes asserted, much as one would assert the unquestioned primacy of personal freedom as a value in American society, the value of instruction in academic reference service. These librarians believe pure and simple that the role of the academic library is to teach. Period. Others disagree and see information services rather than instruction as the role of the academic library. If indeed we are dealing with matters of deeply rooted belief, then the prospects for consensus on this issue equal the prospects for genuine, lasting peace in Northern Ireland.

Jerry Campbell's mission statement for Access Engineers could, as was pointed out in the question-and-answer period after his talk at the Duke Institute, serve as a mission statement for the entire library. It stops short of explicitly calling for a change in the academic library's mission from providing access to information to providing information itself. Yet a number of the participants at the two Institutes (including this participant) see that as a life-and-death matter for the institution we know as the academic library. This is a key issue.

TWO MODELS AND THEIR IMPLICATIONS

The "access to information" model has served academic libraries well. However technology is subverting it with increasing rapidity and will render obsolete those libraries (and librarians) that cling to it. When the library was clearly co-extensive with the building so named, access to information was provided in one place. Anyone who wanted information had access to it through that one place and had to travel to that place to get information. One might call it the Library Most Decidedly With Walls. In this environment the "sit-and-wait" model of reference service served well (or at least well enough). Brief consultations held over reference desks were adequate in the era of the unchallenged dominance of print and the linear methods by which information is stored in and retrieved from print. The advice (or one-to-one instruction) dispensed from the reference desk had a certain cookie-cutter sameness that mirrored the basic similarities among printed reference tools.

However, access to remote information sources, access from remote locations to the library's tools, and the plethora of electronic information systems that have emerged in the past decade challenge this traditional model. They also challenge libraries to devise new ways of providing information services and to redefine what those services ought to be and what users of those services ought to expect from providers. In this new era the reference desk appears, as Virginia Massey-Burzio has noted, like a service that isn't meant to be taken seriously. The increase in options call for a new type of service and we must determine to what extent and in what form that new service model ought to incorporate user instruction. Users of the Library Without Walls ought not to have to come to the Library Most Decidedly With Walls for formal instruction to learn how to use the Library Without Walls. Yet the reality remains that we haven't yet reached the nirvana where everything within the walls is available to those outside, let alone that nirvana where extramural users can reach through those walls without some form of instruction. Two paradigms have informed the development of the academic library; neither fits the technological realities nor the user-centered service goals of the 1990s.

TWO PARADIGMS IN CONFLICT

Ted Nelson, the visionary creator of the terms "hypertext" and "hypermedia" and the revolutionary ideas they symbolize, has identified two paradigms in the design of computer systems. These are applicable to the design of academic library service programs. The first paradigm is what Nelson calls "the technoid vision." He defines it thus:

- We'll have wonderful, wonderful things; and
- they'll get more and more complicated.
- I get credit for this complication, he gets credit for that complication, and we won't even know who created the other complications; and
- you have to learn it the way we're going to stuff it to you, because that is the destiny of technology.[1]

"Sophistication," Nelson says, is part and parcel of the technoid vision. He says "Technoids use sophisticated to mean some curious combination of powerful and complicated; it's practically synonymous with complicated. Theirs is the myth that anything good must be complicated. You cannot become a technoid without breathing this myth deeply into your soul."[2]

The other paradigm is that of the school teacher. Reflecting on how much he hated history in school and how much he enjoyed it when he got out of school and read history on his own, Nelson somewhat cynically describes education as "a system of systematically and serially ruining successive subjects for you."[3] The persona of the school teacher, insistent upon obtaining the right answer from every student, ruined history for Nelson but gave him the image of the second paradigm. The school teacher paradigm values above all else the "correct" answer.

Nelson rightly says a plague on both these houses. He calls instead for a third paradigm which emphasizes individual freedom. He criticizes both of the old paradigms, noting that "The technoids would station *complication* as a barrier between us and freedom. Teachers, and others,

142

would put getting the *correct answer* between us and freedom."[4] He says that "computers can enable freedom."[5] So can academic libraries, through their reference service programs.

THESE PARADIGMS IN THE ACADEMIC LIBRARY

The academic library unquestionably displays many signs of the technoid paradigm. As I wrote on the LIBREF-L listserv shortly before the Berkeley Institute, in response to Lee Jaffee's[6] fundamental question about why libraries offer reference service,

> The library *is* complex. It is a collection of information materials in many formats, some of which cause fragmentation in the order of the collection. The ideal would be for all materials, regardless of format, to be organized in one continuous scheme governed by a classification scheme. For the typical library user, neither the LC nor the Dewey classification scheme fulfills their wishes; both appear to be arbitrary. (People do not, as a rule, organize their personal collections of information sources by LC or Dewey; their collections also have the problem of fragmentation due to different formats' differing storage needs—e.g., books and photocopies, or cookbooks, photocopies and clippings, recipe cards.) This is compounded by the vagaries of library buildings that sometimes dictate undesirable arrangements for organizing materials. Few people (if any) can walk into such an environment and simply find what they want without the assistance of tools. Hence the necessity of our catalogs—catalogs that often insist that users search them by using controlled vocabularies, a concept that does not come naturally to most people. But there is also fragmentation among our tools. To date catalogs rarely provide information about anything other than books and their equivalents (e.g., a video or a sound recording or a manuscript) and serials, the last at the title level rather than the needed article level. So a user generally needs to use more than one finding tool to get to the materials that will fulfill an information need.[7]

In other words, the typical academic library is a *prima facie* manifestation of the technoid paradigm. The school teacher paradigm was imposed atop this paradigm in a well-intentioned effort to ameliorate the problems created for users by the technoid paradigm's multitudinous complexities. If one is looking for evidence supporting the hypothesis that the division on the BI question is a matter of deeply held values and beliefs, one can find no stronger evidence than the strength of many academic librarians' allegience to the school teacher paradigm. The search strategy models promoted in BI sessions are a manifestation of this paradigm. These strategies (e.g., begin with a specialized encyclopedia, then select a handbook for additional background information, look up unfamiliar technical terms in a specialized dictionary, then use one or more specialized periodical indexes) offer users a simple approach to the incredible complexity of the library, a system organized by the technoid complexity paradigm. Unfortunately user needs arise in individual freedom rather than within the neatly circumscribed confines of the school teacher paradigm and many users' individual needs do not fit the search strategies' patterns. As Tom Eadie has noted, "Information gathering made simple is information gathering made superficial."[8]

Further evidence of the strength of the school teacher paradigm in academic reference lies in many librarians' responses to users' manipulation of CD-ROM databases. Librarians' complaints about users' "poor" searches on SilverPlatter databases serve as one example. Some librarians despair over the very broad free-text searches users content themselves with instead of doing carefully crafted Boolean searches combining subject descriptors. In other words, they don't think these users have found what Nelson disparagingly calls "the correct answer." A SilverPlatter® interface that promotes personal freedom would be one that first translates those free-text searches into descriptor-based searches, then models the results of both types of searches in adjacent windows, and finally allows the user to choose between and modify either one. Free users must be left the freedom to choose and to judge the value of the information they receive. Yet at the same time librarians can help them make well-informed judgments, just as better electronic information systems could.

To a great extent, efforts to instruct library users are correctional efforts for systemic problems resulting from the technoid paradigm. The school teacher paradigm informs many of these efforts, but it fails to fit the realities of the complexities. Neither paradigm gives users a central role. Users are victims of both paradigms, poorly served by the complexity of the technoids' paradigm, and found lacking when they are unable to apply the school teacher paradigm to their individual information problems, regardless of whether or not that paradigm fits a particular problem. Nelson's third paradigm promoting personal freedom provides an attractive, viable alternative. The question is how to translate that into service programs in libraries.

The technoid paradigm creates systemic problems for users. Academic libraries have been far too content to accept these problems and "solve" them by making users learn to cope with complexity by finding the "correct" answers; libraries should instead change the systems that created the problems in the first place. No system will be perfect and some degree of instruction will be necessary before users can reap benefit from a system. Yet systems (whether they are programmable VCRs or university libraries) need to be designed to minimize the user's responsibility lest the user become the system's victim. In describing user-centered design of electronic devices and other consumer products, John Sedgwick notes its limits. "User-centered design can go only so far to make a new technological system seem natural, though. Some operations simply have to be learned. For instance, does a computer's UP arrow mean that the text goes up (and the screen down) or the screen goes up (and the text down)? Neither mental model is more intuitive than the other; the correct answer has to be memorized."[9] Surely there are analogs to the "computer's UP arrow" in an academic library; yet academic librarians have not carefully analyzed their operations to determine which things must be memorized and which ought to be incorporated into user-centered designs in such a way that users never have to concern themselves with the latter group.

RESOLUTION TO THE CONFLICTS

Anyone can come into a library and find *something*. Perhaps what a user finds is the best information available; perhaps it is not good enough. However only the user can judge that. But unless the user is made aware of options, he or she cannot make an informed judgment. Because they know more about the universe of available information and information tools than users do, reference librarians, through more in-depth service than a public, crowded, busy reference desk allows for, can make users aware of these options. The librarian can add value to users' information seeking. An example through analogy is helpful:

If I get a sore throat I can soothe it by drinking a lot of hot tea with honey and sucking on throat lozenges. These are the tools/remedies available to me on my own. Or I can go to my physician and describe my problem to him. He then examines me, perhaps takes a throat culture, puts the evidence together, and comes up with a diagnosis and prescribes a course of action to effect a cure. In other words, I take advantage of his medical knowledge. So too, users can generally find *something* on their own. However if they consult with a reference librarian they can take advantage of the librarian's bibliographic knowledge and be offered a course of action that may well be more effective. (Consider the classic "Where is the *Readers' Guide*?" or "Where is the *World Book*?" questions.)

Given the complexity inherent in any library and given that the reference librarian possesses in-depth understanding and knowledge of the bibliographic universe represented by and through the library's collection, the librarian's role is to collaborate with users to the point where they can judge the value of a given item for their particular needs. This has implications for the way in which service is delivered. For example, if a user poses a broad question to find information on subject "X" and the best resource (based on the librarian's professional judgment, a judgment based, of course, on bibliographic knowledge) for fulfilling that need is a periodical index, the user needs to know how to read the citations and how to retrieve the items he or she judges to be relevant.

And this is where we get into the issue that generally passes as "reference philosophy." Do you give them the fish they've asked for or do you teach them to fish so they can do it all on their own the next time? It depends. And that is why I think it is an important principle...that the role of the reference librarian in this collaborative effort with the user is to help that person along to the point of judgment of the value of information and information sources identified. If the user is going to have recurrent needs for that type of information, then teach them to fish for themselves. This will expedite the user's process for getting to that critical judgment point. (Ranganathan's "Save the time of the reader" is another principle that ought to govern the way we do reference and why we do it the way we do it.) If it is going to be a one-time need (as many are), then give them the fish. This may appear to be inconsistent, but I don't think it is. The important thing is to bring together the user and the information sources likely to satisfy the user's need and then let the user judge their value, something only the user can do. How to do that will be highly situation-specific. The important thing is to do it. In some cases the user will have a deeper knowledge of the complexity of the library and the reasons for that complexity—knowledge that can be used in the future. In other cases the user won't know anything about that but it doesn't matter since the need is isolated and an explanation of the complexity would only waste both parties' time.[10]

This approach fits Nelson's new paradigm of the primacy of personal freedom. Users are not forced to learn the complexity of the library or any of its subordinate information systems; nor are they expected to find the correct answer as judged by someone else. It also gives the users their rightful central role in the process and allows them to make the critical judgments.

This approach also fits reality. Too often academic reference librarians approach every query as if it were coming from a doctoral candidate preparing to launch into an exhaustive literature search on a likely dissertation topic. Many needs posed in an academic library are far more circumscribed and each must be judged by its own standard, a standard established by the individual information seeker, not by the librarian.[11] The school teacher paradigm shows no sympathy for the students content with what they judge to be good enough; the inherently unforgiving school teacher paradigm expects each student to make sure that for every need he or she has found the absolute best available. Expecting adherence to this standard is as naive as arguing that no instruction of any sort should be offered because eventually we will reach an information systems nirvana in which every system is so user friendly that no instruction of any kind is needed. SilverPlatter searches that fail to take advantage of the full power of a poorly designed user interface may fail a librarian's standard for good-enough; but they meet the users' standards. Furthermore, Stephen Stoan[12] and Barbara Fister[13] have shown how academic library users actually seek and use information in ways that defy the school teacher paradigm and point towards Nelson's personal freedom paradigm.

Another reality has been articulated by Eadie. As he has put it so forthrightly, user instruction does not work. BI has been undertaken and ambitious programs have been developed for the loftiest of ideals as well as for the most craven of motives. On the one hand, well-intentioned librarians have wanted to enrich students' educational experiences; and on the other, some reference librarians have embraced user education to, as one explained it to me, "ward off reference questions." Several years ago, just after Eadie's article was published, some of the participants in the BI-L listserv reacted to it rather defensively. A lengthy, multi-participant discussion of the value of bibliographic instruction was summarized by one participant who drew an analogy between BI and eating spinach, saying that he valued his work because he knew it could do no harm and might even do some good. The consensus was that the clearest value of BI programs is to increase students' awareness that they can seek assistance from reference librarians. Surely academic librarians are bright enough and creative enough to find other, more efficient, less costly means to achieve this end. For years and years Madison Avenue has successfully made sure that American consumers are aware of the newest kind of soft drink, or automobile, or chewing gum, or body deodorant. We should borrow and apply some of Madison Avenue's mass communication techniques rather than expend so much of our limited, precious professional labor on ineffective instruction programs that yield no more benefit than can be achieved through effective advertising.

Once self-assured about the centrality of instruction to the academic library's mission, at least some user instruction advocates are beginning to display symptoms of confusion. The BI-L self-assessment of their efforts as nothing grander than public awareness ought to be cause for serious reflection. A recent position announcement posted to the LIBREF-L listserv on behalf of Utica College of Syracuse University called for a reference and BI librarian described thus: "Creative, forward-looking, service-oriented public services librarian is sought. The successful candidate will participate as a member of a team that will be implementing the 'new' reference paradigm. This person will take a leadership role in creating and developing an appropriate bibliographic instruction program that takes into account the changing nature of reference."[14] This statement is tellingly vague about what the new paradigm is, how the nature of reference is changing, or what sort of instruction is appropriate to it. It is symptomatic of the confusion the participants in the Institutes experienced. It also demonstrates the difficulty in letting go of an old paradigm and making the transition to the new. Instruction is so part and parcel of the procrustean school teacher paradigm that many will have difficulty envisioning a new paradigm in which instruction's role is either greatly diminished or non-existent.

Ultimately, user instruction crashes to pieces between the Scylla of the technoid paradigm and the Charybdis of the school teacher paradigm. Individual users, thus left adrift by failed collective solutions that ignore their individual needs, need something different. The collaborative relationship discussed above in which the librarian's response fits the individual user's need fits the new paradigm. However, as Campbell has pointed out, academic library budgets won't allow for intensive interpersonal interaction between a reference librarian and every user.

THE FUTURE

Meanwhile, reference librarians—participants at both institutes agreed—need to be involved in system design and redesign, both in their own institutions and in the marketplace of commercial systems, to bring us and our users closer to that nirvana that definitely does not exist today. Although instruction may be needed today to compensate for system shortcomings, as well as for those things (yet to be definitively identified) that simply *must* be learned, librarians must start to think and speak in terms of the new paradigm. Doing so can help it become a self-fulfilling prophecy as practitioners throughout the field become more and more comfortable with it.

"In a little book of 1911 entitled *An Introduction to Mathematics*, the English philosopher and scientist Alfred North Whitehead pointed out that 'civilization advances by extending the number of important operations we can perform without thinking about them.'"[15] Information retrieval ought to be one of those operations, working in service of information delivery. If the mission of the academic library becomes delivery of information, then it becomes even more imperative that user instruction in access and retrieval techniques be kept to a minimum lest resources be diverted from the mission. There may not be consensus that this ought to be the mission of the academic library; however in an environment in which organizations such as Prodigy, Compuserve, and America Online provide information delivery with a minimum of instruction in information access and retrieval techniques, academic libraries need to take notice, spot this clear trend, and capitalize on it.

The complexity of the only systems available until recently (including the very complex, seemingly arbitrary academic library) has allowed many academic librarians to focus their energy on teaching users about that complexity and encouraging them to find and apply "the correct answer" when using it. The mechanics of information retrieval rather than the evaluation of information retrieved has been the bread and butter of bibliographic instruction programs, even despite recent talk about "information literacy." Many academic librarians have, in other words, invested great effort into teaching library users about things that library users ought to be able to do without thinking about them. However since insufficient effort has been invested into modifying information systems so they can be used as if they are second nature, users are the victims of unresolved systemic problems. The best hope is to devise tools that will allow them to turn the inherent liabilities of the library built on the technoid paradigm into plusses, enabling them to gather information easily and to receive it from any of innumerable sources where they want it, when they want it, in the format they want it.

Systems development will inevitably bring virtual reality to information systems and academic libraries. This offers as much peril as promise. If in a virtual reality universe we replicate the library built on the technoid model, we will have wasted more of our scarce personnel resources than we have wasted developing the school teacher bibliographic instruction paradigm. We need new metaphors in a hypertext, hypermedia world. To replicate systems that use seemingly arbitrary classification schemes and controlled vocabularies will not benefit our users. We need to seek meta-metaphors for information. The metaphor of the library, that is the library as a place and a discrete physical entity, cannot survive that transition. Nor will there be any predetermined "correct answers" nor any universally applicable search strategies. Each user will shape and reshape the information landscape to meet individual needs. To get there, we academic librarians must get beyond their current impasse on the "To BI or not to BI?" question and recognize that its answer is almost always individual and situational. And we need to commit ourselves to designing systems that, as much as possible, allow users to retrieve information without thinking about information retrieval. We need to begin moving on to the new paradigm of maximum individual freedom.

1   Theodor Nelson, "Freedom and Power." In G. R. Boynton and Sheila D. Creth, *New Technologies and New Directions: Proceedings from the Symposium on Scholarly Communication, The University of Iowa, November 14-16, 1991*, p. 2. (Westport, CT: Meckler, 1993).

2   ibid., p. 3.

3   ibid., p. 4.

4   ibid., p. 5. Italics in original.

5   ibid.

6   Lee Jaffee, communication to LIBREF-L listserv at KENTVM, 25 February 1993.

7   James Rettig, communication to LIBREF-L listserv at KENTVM, 25 February 1993.

8   Tom Eadie, "Immodest Proposals: User Instruction for Students Does Not Work," *Library Journal* 115 (October 15, 1990): 45.

9   John Sedgwick, "The Complexity Problem," *Atlantic* 271 (March 1993): 96

10 James Rettig, communication to LIBREF-L listserv at KENTVM, 25 February 1993.

11 For more on my views of the role of the individual information seeker vis-a-vis the librarian's and the centrality of judging in the information process, see James Rettig, "Self-Determining Information Seekers," *RQ* 32 (Winter 1992), 158-63.

12 Stephen K. Stoan, "Research and Library Skills: An Analysis and Interpretation," *College & Research Libraries* 45 (March 1984): 99-109.

13 Barbara Fister, "The Research Process for Undergraduate Students," *Journal of Academic Librarianship* 18 (July 1992): 163-69.

14 Raul A. Huerta, communication to LIBREF-L listserv at KENTVM, 11 June 1993.

15 Charles Scribner, Jr., *In the Web of Ideas* (New York: Charles Scribner's Sons, 1993), p. 89.

PART II: THE PROCESS

Anne G. Lipow and Lou Wetherbee

16. PRINCIPLES

17. IMPLEMENTING THE PRINCIPLES

18. TIPS FOR REPLICATING THE INSTITUTE

19. MAJOR COST COMPONENTS

This section covers the thinking, the components, and the steps that went into preparing for the Institute. We hope that this level of detail will assist others who wish to organize "rethinking" sessions in their local libraries or regions. As much as possible, we try to "pull back the curtain" and describe what we had in mind in choosing a particular discussion format or sequence of activities.

16. PRINCIPLES

Above all, we strived for a highly relevant, stimulating, and smoothly-run program with few disappointments. Adhering to the following five principles helped to attain these objectives.

1. Be clear about the goals of the program, and recruit participants compatible with those goals.

    *   Leadership and good ideas can come from anywhere; give serious consideration to recruiting from throughout the library hierarchy.

2. Have realistic expectations about inventiveness and behavioral change.

    *   Creative thinking comes easier to most people when they know something about the topic in question.

    *   Changing old ways of thinking and doing requires time and practice; such change cannot be expected to happen after one lecture or one day of training.

    *   It is easier for participants to share what they experienced and learned if they are supplied with written material that supports the program.

3. Meet audience expectations; shape some of them.

    *   People do best when they know what to expect, when there are no surprises, when there is a logic to the sequence and content of the program.

    *   Presenters must not only know their material but also be competent, interesting oral speakers; instructors must be effective teachers.

    *   Expect the unexpected; reduce surprises: prepare for "What can go wrong."

    *   You can't and won't make all participants happy all of the time, but aim to make all participants happy some of the time.

    *   With the best of planning, some things will go differently from what you had planned. Use an effective evaluation mechanism and pay attention to suggestions and criticisms in your repeat offerings of the program.

    *   Audiences generally complain if they don't receive copies of a speaker's overhead transparencies.

4. Facilitate participants' ability to absorb and use the content of the program through structure and pacing.

   • An apparent structure to the program helps to keep everyone moving forward together.

   • Good pacing will keep participants alert and create a senses of momentum. Intersperse different types of activities: active and passive, hard and easy, thinking and doing, sitting and moving, talking and silence, work and play (serious and frivolous), small groups and plenary sessions.

   • People take in new information in different ways. Aim to provide a variety of presentational methods early in the program to ensure that as many of those ways as possible are addressed.

   • The more senses an adult uses in the learning task, the longer what was learned will stick and the more likely it will be put into practice.

5. Exceed audience expectations.

   • Participants' initial attitudes about the program are affected by their earliest contacts with the program; ensure that those contacts are trouble free and highly responsive.

   • It's the little things that count: wherever feasible, provide "added value" accommodations.

17. IMPLEMENTING THE PRINCIPLES

1. Be clear about the goals of the program, and recruit participants compatible with those goals.

   The Institute organizers, both of whom work regularly with libraries of all types throughout the country, observed that library personnel were coping on a day-to-day basis with some difficult issues and pressures with no good sources of guidance, largely because they were breaking new ground. The goal of the program, then, was **not** to come up with definitive answers—it was too early for that. Rather it was to provide those who were dealing with the problems time to stand back and think, talk, question, and bounce new ideas off people in similar situations. To ensure a group of participants in similar situations—that is, who dealt with relatively homogeneous issues—and to narrow the range of expertise required of Institute speakers and instructors, the Institute focused on academic libraries. Within those boundaries, however, it was important not to exclude any level of personnel who played a part in shaping their library's future.

Therefore, the title of the Institute and the descriptive publicity specified the audience for whom this program was intended. From the announcement:

"Rethinking Reference: New Models and How to Get There"

Focus: Reference services in academic libraries

Audience: Library managers and others who influence their reference services.

2. Have realistic expectations about inventiveness and behavioral change.

Time is precious for library workers. Their difficulty in getting away from the office is often the reason given for providing only half-day or even one-day educational programs on topics that are essential to affecting participants' thinking or behavior. Within days after a workshop, participants are doing their work just as they had before the workshop; chances are slim that they are using what they learned. Such workshops are, for practical purposes, a waste of time.

We wanted the Institute experience to be more than an academic exercise. To provide the time it would take for participants to be willing and able to take action back home after the program, we did three things:

(a) The length of the program was scheduled for 2-1/2 days:

Friday evening: 7:00-10:00 pm

Saturday: 7:30 am-5:30 pm

Sunday: 7:30 am-3:00 pm

We received a few complaints about scheduling the program on a weekend. Most workers do not appreciate spending their weekends on work-related activities. To hold this program during the week, however, would have increased airfare for registrants from afar, thereby prohibitively increasing the registrants' expenses. Once this was explained, people understood and favored the lower cost over a weekday scheduling. (For programs where only local registrants are expected and airfares are not an issue, scheduling the program during the workweek should be given serious consideration. Expect complaints from people who feel they cannot take work time off for such activity. Best of all worlds is if you can plan repeat programs and hold some during the week and some on the weekend.)

(b) Enrollees were asked to do some background reading before coming to the Institute, and to complete a writing assignment and turn it in three weeks before the start of the Institute. (See Appendix A)

Putting enrollees to work before the start of the Institute, in effect extended its length by several hours. The readings were intended to bring all participants to a common baseline of exposure to ideas about change and the future of libraries; the writing assignment was designed to give participants a head start in thinking about the issues that would be discussed. Participation in the Institute could be expected to begin at a more advanced level than might have been possible without the assignments. Respectful of enrollees' time pressures, we tried to convey that however much or little time they could spend on the assignment would be worth their while. Since we would make everyone's written assignment available to the rest of the group, others would be benefitting from their thinking. Participants commented in their evaluations that the readings and homework assignments were quite useful in helping them get into the mental swing of the Institute. Many shared the readings and assignment with their fellow staff and came to the Institute having the benefit of their colleagues' input. Such early involvement of library staff sealed a commitment to continue discussions after the Institute.

(c) We used e-mail extensively both before and after the institute to create a conference network environment and to extend and reinforce the Institute experience. (It would have been far more effective to provide a discussion bulletin service, but such an arrangement was not feasible.) E-mail was used to communicate "housekeeping" details, transmit articles already in electronic form, receive participants' pre-Institute assignments, distribute post-Institute information. The four or five participants who did not have e-mail addresses received the communications by regular post.

3. Meet audience expectations; shape some of them.

A preliminary agenda was mailed to participants before the program; the final agenda was included in their packets which was given to them upon registration.

Written material that supported the oral presentations was made available; each participant had printed instructions explaining each small-group task; group leaders were given printed instructions that supported an oral orientation. Even the small-group outcomes reported at the end of one day were amalgamated, reproduced and distributed first thing the next day. This capability required a handy portable computer, printer, and copier/stapler as well as staff who worked late into the evening. Small-group outcomes reported at the end of the program were amalgamated and sent to participants within a week or two after the program.

The speakers we chose were all experienced thinkers or achievers in their special areas. Several were nationally known, having written seminal articles or given highly successful presentations on their topics.

A handy copier was essential to comply promptly with the audience's wish to have copies of one of the speakers' overhead transparencies that hadn't been included in their packets.

We kept extra handouts, name badges and packets (for those who lose or forget, as well as for the person who registered but who got dropped from our records!).

We arranged with the conference facilities to have a troubleshooter on call.

The evaluation technique used for this program was called a TALKBACK— a one-hour plenary session that asked participants to comment on any aspect of the program they chose, but also on particular aspects which were listed on an easel. There are several advantages to an open evaluation over a written one: each participant as well as all of the staff heard what others got out of the program, which often triggered their own thoughts. They also learned that what displeased one person was the highlight of the program for another person.

Because of suggestions made in the evaluations of the Berkeley Institute, a few changes were made in the Duke program: as mentioned in another context, the speaker on "the change process" was moved to an earlier slot, which indeed improved the logic and pacing of the proceedings. Also, because of the popular reception to the ideas presented by two of the Berkeley participants, the two attended the Duke institute as part of the staff, thus ensuring that their issues were included in that program.

4. Facilitate the audience's ability to absorb and use the content of the program through structure and pacing.

The reasoning that underlay the sequence of activities in the Berkeley program was as follows:

- Begin with a keynote speaker who provides a new perspective, the "big picture," mold-shattering ideas
- Next, provide current information:
  – Case studies of innovative change in particular libraries
  – Major controversial issues and emerging patterns of change
- Then, leaving librarianship for the moment, teach about the process of change, what make it go better or worse and why Finally, let participants go at the task of brainstorming about the future of reference and how we might begin to move in new directions.

Logical as that design seemed in the planning stages, in practice it had a flawed structure. In the program evaluation, participants suggested that the instruction session on the change process be moved to the beginning of the program so that they could make earlier use of the new concepts and vocabulary they learned in that class. As can be seen by comparing the two agendas (see Appendix), the Duke program complied with this recommendation, with faultless results.

Except for the keynote speaker and the instructor in "the process of change," all presenters spoke very briefly: 5, 15, or 20 minutes. (Shorter speeches force tighter, more information-packed, livelier content.) The 5-minute talks, an innovation at the Duke Institute only, were "infomercials" that gave the audience a reason for joining the speaker in small-group discussion later. The 15- and 20-minute talks were followed by plenary discussions.

159

Each participant was assigned to small 9-12 person discussion groups that met throughout the weekend. The sum membership in each group represented as much diversity in background and experience as could be managed: small, medium, and large libraries; front-line librarians, middle management, and top administrators; male and female; generalists and specialists. These groups conducted structured business, came to consensus, and reported their results in plenary sessions.

The Institutes were limited to 60 or so participants for two reasons:
(a) to maximize individual involvement (groups larger than 12— including staff—are not conducive to full membership participation); and

(b) to make efficient use of our limited time together (more than seven groups reporting their results at the plenary session takes more time than can be afforded and usually results in repetitive content).

Each participant was also assigned to a "buddy" group: homogeneous small groups of 3-4 people who had one or more of the following in common: size of library, level of responsibility, subject specialty. These groups began meeting at the start of the program. Their purpose was to break the ice, enable people who knew no one at the outset to feel less like a stranger, and to the extent that the groupings were congenial, foster longer-term relationships of support that might extend beyond the Institute.

The "soapbox" discussion groups were an opportunity for participants to join whichever groups they liked. (See Appendix D)

Participants moved in and out of a steady succession of lectures, plenary discussion, small group discussion, exercises with outcomes, meals and informal discussion, unstructured group discussions. They read, they wrote, they talked, they disagreed, they came to consensus. They were exposed to new information about mostly familiar territory, but also to new information about an unfamiliar topic: The change process. The newness of this material, the expertise of the instructor, and the fact that the instructor was a consultant from outside the library profession combined to stretch minds and stimulate new directions of thought. Several participants had the opportunity to lead discussions and give short presentations before the full audience.

Participants who were reluctant to join in discussion in a large group had several opportunities to share their ideas in different types of small groups:

• 12-member discussion group—had structured assignments, with their results reported to the plenary session. Each group had a leader from among the participants and at least one Institute staff member assigned to assist. Part of the experience to be gained in this group was the achievement of coming to consensus. Since such an endeavor takes effort and practice, participants stayed with the same group throughout the weekend.

• 4-member buddy group—very informal; no pressure to continue the group if it didn't work out. Soapboxes—8 or 9 fluid "hot topic" discussion groups, which participants moved in and out of depending on their personal interests. In addition to the pre-established soapbox topics, both at Berkeley and Duke, *ad hoc* soapboxes, led by a participant proponent of the topic, were added to respond to key issues raised at the moment.

5. Exceed audience expectations.

Knowing that attention to detail is both appreciated and regarded as a measure of the quality of the program, considerable effort went into providing every convenience:

• The Institute offered Berkeley enrollees the opportunity to make dinner reservations at Chez Panisse, a world-renowned restaurant with no last-minute vacancies.

• The Institute offered to pair Duke registrants who wanted to room with someone else but didn't know other registrants.

• At both programs, a highly selective guide to restaurants was included in packets.

• At Duke, participants were given the opportunity to attend a special orientation to the Triangle Research Libraries Network, the oldest library cooperative network in the country.

• The conference facilities were ample, comfortable, and attractive; they were within easy walking distance from participants' lodgings, sometimes in the same building.

161

- All participants received a commemorative T-shirt with a cartoon drawn by the well-known librarian-satirist Gary Handman.

- Packets included a roster of participants—which made follow-up contact easy.

- Name badges were the sort that hangs around the neck like a pendant (which most conference goers prefer). Other types of badges were available, but no one opted for them.

- Meals were delicious, varied, and accommodated vegetarian choices; breaks included good pastries.

- Writing tablets and writing utensils were provided.

- Directional signs were posted at ambiguous junctures to all meeting rooms, and meeting rooms were clearly labeled.

17. TIPS FOR REPLICATING THE INSTITUTE

While this format will work within a single institution, the synergy present by combining participants from many institutions is a good reason to seek a collaborative method when trying to replicate it locally. Some specific ideas that can help make the Institute a success are:

- Organizing Committee.—Create a small core group of very interested individuals willing to invest some time and energy in adapting the schedule to the local environment.

- Agenda.—Study the different agendas as presented at Berkeley and Duke, and develop an understanding of the various activities and their role in creating a participative, engaging learning environment. Provide adequate time for informal socializing and breaks to minimize participants' fatigue.

- Keynote. Choose a local "keynote" presenter who can motivate and challenge the participants (the role played by Jerry Campbell). This component is very important. If a single presenter is not possible, consider a debate format to engender high interest and to spur discussion.

- Change Process. Use a consultant experienced in explaining the steps in organizational change, or design a small group exercise which will involve the participants in considering the factors that tend to promote change in organizations.

- **Role of Facilitator.** Select a facilitator to guide the participants through the process, maintain focus, keep the discussion periods well-organized, and ensure that participants understand the small-group tasks. The facilitator should also meet with small-group representatives to provide them with guidance in how to summarize the outcomes of their groups for review and discussion in the larger group. It is the facilitator's responsibility to ensure that everyone has a fair chance to be heard and that no one person or small group dominates the session.

- **Purpose of Small Group Tasks.** Review the small group tasks in this book and adjust or adapt them to your schedule. They should follow the presentation of the "content" material presented early in the schedule. Task 1 is designed to promote creative thought about the "pieces" or "components" of the new reference. It also has a sub-task aimed at helping participants identify services that can be ended or phased out. Task 2 is designed to provide participants with practical ideas they can take back and implement in their local environments. Whoever develops the small-group tasks must be familiar with the content of the program and modify the tasks to meet local needs.

- **Small-Group Process.** Provide flipcharts or overhead transparencies and give the small groups clear written instructions about how to record their discussions. The facilitator should repeat the instructions and answer questions just prior to breaking into groups. Small-groups will need to select or appoint a facilitator, figure out how to record discussion, and set ground rules for breaking log-jams. The facilitator can make suggestions, summarize, and guide toward closure, but should not otherwise intervene unless so requested by members of the group. Optimum group size is 8-10 persons.

- **Discussion Periods.** Provide plenty of time for discussions in the assembled large group. Institute participants like hearing what everyone has to say and what everyone else is hearing, so balance the small groups with lots of large group-interactive sessions.

- **Buddies.** If participants do not know each other well, you may wish to assign "buddies" as an ice breaker at the opening session of the Institute, but don't force too much togetherness!

- **Soapboxes.** The soapbox sessions are not to be confused with roundtables. They are more fluid and informal. Participants may drop in and out of soapboxes as their interests dictate. The topics should reflect whatever the institute organizers feel are the issues participants will want to grapple with. With easels and pads annotated with names of topics, demarcate spots around a very large room for each soapbox. Provide a few chairs and plenty of space at each soapbox for participants to arrange themselves as they wish. Let spontaneous soapboxes be formed if there is interest. Provide an "open soapbox" for participants to talk about hot topics that emerge after the institute has been planned. This is the place for participants to get passionate about the topics of interest to them without having to stick to a rigid structure.

Trouble-prevention measures:

- Appoint a timekeeper who will warn speakers 2 minutes before their time is up and who will be ruthless in requiring them to stop when their time is up. This person should sit in a spot quite visible to the speakers. Appoint an "air traffic controller" who will take steps to rectify a stuffy, hot, cold, or otherwise uncomfortable room.

- Appoint someone to sit at the back of the room and hold up a special sign as a signal to a speaker who is talking too softly.

18. MAJOR COST COMPONENTS

- Publicity
    Design
    Printing
    Mailing
- Facilities rental
    Large hall for plenary sessions and soapbox sessions
    Breakout rooms for small groups
    Meals and refreshments for breaks
- Staffing fees
    Facilitators
    Speakers
    Aides
- Staff expenses:

Transportation (Air and ground)
Meals, including those additional to meals provided at Institute
Lodging
- Photocopying
    Pre-Institute materials
    Institute packet materials
    Materials produced during the Institute
    Post-Institute materials
- Mailing
    Stamps and envelopes for confirming registrations
    Stamps and packaging for pre-Institute mailings
    Stamps and packaging for post-Institute mailings
- Supplies:
    Easel stand, rent or purchase: one for each small group
        or soapbox
    Easel pads, one for each easel stand
    Flow pens (marking pens for easel pads)
    Lined tablets, one for each participant
    Pens or pencils for participants
    Blank transparencies
    Name badges
    Transparency pens for each group
    Packet folders
    Masking tape

- Equipment:
    Overhead projector and screen
    Microphone at speaker podium
    Cassette tape recorder if proceedings are recorded
    Laptop computer to record small group outcomes
    Access to printer and photocopy machines (preferably with
        automatic collating and stapling capability

- Miscellaneous
    Fees to credit-card firms if charge-card payments are allowed
    T-shirts or other commemorative giveaways
    Telephone and fax expenses

APPENDIX A

STARTING THE INSTITUTE BEFORE
THE SCHEDULED DATE

20. A WELCOME LETTER

21. PRE-INSTITUTE ASSIGNMENT

22. EXAMPLES OF HOMEWORK CONTRIBUTIONS

It was possible and important to extend the length of the Institute by putting the participants to work before the scheduled date. This approach increased participants' readiness to delve into the issues at the very start of the program. The "Welcome Letter" on the next page, in addition to providing the content of an opening communication with participants, describes the ways they were asked to begin preparing for the Institute a few weeks in advance. Next follows the text of their pre-Institute homework assignment. Finally, the homework contributions of two participants—Janice Koyama, Assistant University Librarian for Public Services at UCLA; and Johannah Sherrer, then Head of Reference at Duke, a short time later Library Director at Lewis & Clark—are reproduced as examples of participants' willingness to brainstorm on paper, to risk sharing incomplete thoughts.

20. A WELCOME LETTER

Dear Rethinkers:

A sincere welcome to the upcoming Rethinking Reference Institute! Fresh in my mind is the March presentation at Berkeley of this same program, so I can promise you a most stretching, stimulating, and somewhat exhausting experience.

1. This is the first of 7 e-mail messages that will follow in succession. They are intended to help you prepare for the Institute.

    The next ones are:

    #2: Pre-Institute Assignment

    #3: Selected Readings

    Then follow 4 messages containing texts of articles.

    In mid-May, one more article will be e-mailed to you. Please let me know if somehow any didn't reach you and I'll resend.

2. Dress at the entire Institute is casual — jeans are definitely acceptable.

3. This week we're sending you by regular mail a packet that contains a preliminary program agenda and a map with directions for how to get to the campus and hotels traveling by plane, train, or car. Also enclosed are copies of the hard-to-get articles asterisked in the "Selected Readings" bibliography (memo #3).

Anne

21. PRE-INSTITUTE ASSIGNMENT

To: *Rethinking Reference* participants
Subject: Pre-Institute Assignment

One of the key goals of the Institute is to provide a collaborative environment in which all participants can learn from each other and work together to create practical strategies for change. Your part in achieving this goal is, of course, critical. The assignment below is intended to give you a start in contributing to the collaborative process.

Instructions:

- Choose **at least one** (1) of the 3 options below.
- Each option should be limited in length to **one** page; two pages **max**!!
- **Deadline**: May 21

Send your completed assignment by one of the following routes:

[Instructions for sending by post, e-mail, and fax appeared here.]

Your collective papers will be reproduced and distributed in a packet to all participants at the opening of the Institute. The packet will provide speakers and participants with discussion points and will serve as a resource to the work groups who will define new models of reference service and devise action plans.

Remember, your paper must be received before May 21 to be included in the packet. Thank you!

(continued)

THE ASSIGNMENT:

As you consider any of the 3 options below, keep in mind the needs and effect on these categories of people:

    current clients/library users
    potential clients/library users
    reference service librarians
    library director and senior library administrators
    heads of reference departments
    support staff
    technical services staff
    allies/partners/competitors outside the library

and on these categories of activities:

    collection development
    training

OPTION 1

Draw a library organization chart that represents a new way of handling the reference function— *i.e.*, departs from the traditional public service/technical service structure.
In a brief paragraph or two, describe the changes addressed by your new organization.

OPTION 2

Jot down your ideas about the following issues (be brief, specific, and descriptive; key words/outline/column format is OK; no need to justify):

a.   What new roles will emerge for academic reference staff— both professional and support personnel? What roles will disappear?

b.   Who are the clients of the academic reference department in a networked environment, and where will they be served?

c.   What kinds of training or re-training is needed to help reference staff make the transition to networked information services?

d.   What are the key characteristics of reference departments that are making a successful transition? What have they done?

OPTION 3

Recognizing that change is necessary but budgets are limited, jot down your ideas for moving toward change within the constraints of no more money and no new staff.

EXAMPLES OF HOMEWORK CONTRIBUTIONS

On the following pages, examples of completed pre-Institute assignments are reproduced with the permission of the two authors. Both papers address "Option 2." As in the other cases in this book of "snapshots of thinking", the reader is reminded that these papers represent the authors' hastily written, off-the-top-of-the-head thoughts. —Editor

From: Janice Koyama   Tue, 09 Mar 93 13:55 PST
Subject: LATE: Institute assignment

OPTION 2

a) new roles that will emerge
- librarians will not only be navigators, but creators of ref. tools
- librarians will work with other campus information providers to teach/train staff/users
- librarians and prof. staff will engage in more tutoring, in-house training, in order to prepare for a mix of staffing at the traditional ref. desk and in basic levels of BI
- aca. lib. staff in public services need to be involved with recruitment into library school and support diversity and pipeline initiatives
- better referral mechanisms will be developed and implemented; ref. staff more conscious of how/what to give to users that empowers them in a centralized lib. environment; how to be an effective trainer/user educator using state of the art instructional technology (televideo to remote sites, multi-media); we talk about new information technology and occasionally use microlabs and demos, but we do not rely in a major way on the very technology we talk about to deliver the instructional package

b) who are the clients; where will they be served?
- in addition to primary campus users, we will have more indirect users over Internet who will be able to "see" how our campus selects information to put on a gopher server for example; how

(continued)

we construct databases and searching engines (making more visible ref. tools like quality of cataloging by campus was exposed by shared and cooperative cataloging over the bibliographic networks)

- clients in a networked environment might be "unseen"—no interaction or visual cues to tell you if the "interview" is going well;
- our public service responses will have to be responsive/timely/intelligible/meaningful over a network and this environment will establish new standards for style, content, how to deliver an information response package

c) training/re-training
- more formalized, required attendance at in-house training programs; localized certification?
- more rotations within the library and among campus information providers;
- off desk time devoted to aspects of information technology akin to what time was allotted to learn new indexing and ref. tools, *e.g.,*. appearance of citation indexes

d) key characteristics of ref. depts.
- continuing support for staff development and continuing education
- willingness to define service niches
- ability to disaggregate monolithic client/user groups in order to focus services and programs
- willingness to support experiments and deal with failures
- entrepreneurship/intrapreneurship
- willingness to devote time to planning and evaluation
- ability to organize systematic user input and act responsively to user-initiated service and program ideas
- emphasis on teamwork effort and a reward system that recognizes collaboration

Date: Fri, 28 May 93 12:33:56 EST
From: Johannah Sherrer

a) New Roles:
  More responsibility for actual document delivery
  Will become system advisors
  Assist clients in setting up their own information gateways to
    databases relevant to their needs
  Will give more technical assistance
  Will do more off-site work

  Fading Roles:
  Bibliographic Instruction
  Compiling bibliographies
  Collection Development

b) The client base will expand beyond the immediate university
   community to include all academic clientele, or even the general
   public, and they will be served anywhere the client chooses to
   be served.

c) Must become more technically skilled but not necessarily more
   than the public itself needs to become. But the way we seek
   information or search for it is changing. The strategies are
   changing as well as the sources.
   Trial by error is better than waiting for formal instruction, plus it
   will be the method of choice for the user, more than likely. Staff
   training will be continuous, with the responsibility for that
   training shared EQUALLY by management and staff.

d) Key characteristics of successful Reference Departments:
   Flexible; goal driven rather than task driven; creative; willing to
   risk letting go of traditional practices in order to substitute new
   services; committed to service on the patron's terms; communicate with each other as well as they communicate with patrons;
   team oriented yet independent; resilient; comfortable with change
   and impreciseness; constantly willing to challenge the status quo.

(continued)

What have they done: they don't wait!!!!!
   they make mistakes and profit from them
   they think, talk and write about the future
   they are different from their colleagues at other institutions
   they are looking beyond the profession or to other professions for
      ideas and jumping-off points
   they challenge so-called standards
   they have decreased staff and increased the use of technology
   they have impacted other library departments

APPENDIX B

SELECTED READINGS

23 • RETHINKING REFERENCE: A BIBLIOGRAPHY

Prepared by Anne G. Lipow

The earliest version of this list was sent, along with several of the hard-to-obtain texts (with the authors' permission), to Berkeley participants in early January 1993. It was revised and sent to Duke participants in early April 1993; and it was revised again in August 1993, with contributions from Institute participants, for inclusion in this book. • *Editor*

The full texts of references marked with an asterisk (*) follow this bibliography.

THE FUTURE OF THE REFERENCE DESK

1. Ford, Barbara. "Reference beyond (and without) the reference desk." *College and Research Libraries*, vol. 47, Sept. 1986, 491.
    Questions the reference desk as the central mode of serving clients.

2.* Lipow, Anne G. "21st century job description." Message broadcast to the Visions network discussion group in August 1992.
    Depicts a remotely accessible reference desk.

3. Massey-Burzio, Virginia. et al. "Reference encounters of a different kind: a symposium." *Journal of Academic Librarianship*, vol. 18, no. 5, Nov. 1992, 276.
    Discusses the process of eliminating the reference desk at Brandeis, and 4 other authors respond.

4. Oberg, Larry. "Response to Hammond: Paraprofessionals at the reference desk: the end of the debate." *The Reference Librarian*, no. 37, 1992.
   Urges professionals to break away from the idea of desk duty as a key reason for being.

NEW ROLES FOR LIBRARIES AND LIBRARY PERSONNEL

5. Campbell, Jerry D. "It's a tough job looking ahead when you've seen what's dragging behind." *Journal of Academic Librarianship*, vol. 17, no. 3, 148.

   Argues for rethinking our mission.

6. Campbell, Jerry D. "Shaking the conceptual foundations of reference: a perspective." *Reference Services Review*, Winter 1992, 29.
   Foresees new roles and titles for reference librarians based on a new economic model of providing information to users.

7. Creth, Sheila D. "Creating a virtual information organization: collaborative relationships between libraries and computing centers." *Journal of Library Administration*, Vol. 19, 3/4, 1994. In press.
   Thorough discussion of the need for librarians to enter into collaborative (as opposed to cooperative) relations with campus computing center professionals, as well as strategies for forming successful partnerships.

8. Dougherty, Richard M. "Editorial: Exercising our options." *Journal of Academic Librarianship*, March 1993, 3.
   A call to move from talk to action.

9. Euster, Joanne. "Take charge of the future now." *C&RL News*, Feb. 1993, 89-90.

10. Gorman, Michael. "Making our own luck: Parts 1 and 2." *California Libraries*, February and April, 1993.

11. Holderness, Mike. "Time to shelve the library?" *New Scientist,* Dec. 5, 1992, 22-23.

    At least one person's view that there will be no role at all for libraries; that libraries are becoming increasingly irrelevant to all except "historians of the pre-computer age."

12.* Lipow, Anne G. "Reorganization in reference departments: summary of responses." Distributed on LIBREF-L and LIBADMIN listservs January 6, 1992.

    Summary of 20 responses to request for descriptions of innovative reorganization in reference services or redefined positions within reference department.

13. Malinconico, Michael. "Information's brave new world." *Library Journal,* May 1, 1992, 36.

    Premise: New developments could displace librarians or magnify their importance; librarians can deny change or anticipate it and exploit it to their advantage.

14. Myers, Judy E., Thomas C. Wilson and John H. Lienhard. "Surfing the sea of stories: riding the information revolution." *Mechanical Engineering,* vol. 114, no. 10, Oct. 1992, 60.

15. Oberg, Larry. "The emergence of the paraprofessional in academic libraries: perceptions and realities. *College and Research Libraries,* March 1992, 100.

    Bases conclusion that new model of librarianship is needed on the growing ambiguity between the roles of paraprofessionals and librarians.

16. Smith, Eldred. "The print prison." *Library Journal,* Feb. 1, 1992.

    Argues that electronic information technology provides the means to overcome print's limitations, and suggests new roles for collection development and reference librarians in academic libraries.

17. "Staff versus collections: assessing budget priorities for the 1990s." A symposium of articles by Jerry Campbell, Patrick O'Brien, and Sheila Creth. *Library Administration & Management*, Summer 1992, 126.

    The 3 authors differ in their assessment of budget priorities in affecting change, but they agree that to survive, libraries cannot continue the status quo.

18.* Strategic Visions Steering Committee. "Strategic Vision for Professional Librarians" and "Values and Qualities of Librarianship."

    Draft documents prepared in January 1992, distributed on the Visions listserv, and at regional professional meetings.

19. Tiffany, Constance J. "Tiered services or tiered constituencies." *California Libraries*, Vol. 3, no. 3, March 1993, p. 1.

20. Wainwright, Eric. "The intermediaries perspective: the role of libraries in an electronic world." *Australian Academic and Research Libraries*, vol. 24, no. 1, March 1993, 30-33.

    Cogent examination of the role and underlying assumptions of the traditional university library and how those must change in an electronic information environment.

21.* Willis, Alfred and Eugene Matysek. "Place and functionality of reference services from the perspective of TQM theory." *LIBRES* [electronic journal], August 1992.

PERSPECTIVES ON CHANGE

Read whatever you can on the process of organizational change and how to help others move through it constructively. Some authors that give useful information, advice, and perspectives on change are:

22. Adams, James L. "Conceptual Blockbusting" and "The Care and Feeding of Ideas" COMPLETE REFERENCES

23. Goldberg, Beverly. "Manage Change—Not the Chaos Caused by Change." *Management Review*, Nov. 1992.

24. Kanter, Rosabeth Moss. Her numerous articles on change

25. Seligman, Martin E. P. *Learned Optimism: How to Change Your Mind and Your Life*. New York: Knopf, 1991.

26. May, Rollo. "Courage to Create." New York: Norton, 1975.

The following bibliography is #16 in the series "NASA Program/Project Management Resource List." It appeared on the Visions listserv 16 June 1993, and is reproduced here with permission of the author, Jeffrey Michaels, Program/Project Management Librarian, NASA Headquarters Library, Washington, D.C. —Editor

VISION AND STRATEGIC PLANNING

Revised June 1993

Introduction

Some of the following authors will tell you that organizational planning of any kind is most successful when a vision is in place first. Definitions of vision vary, but in Charles Handy's The Age of Unreason there is the following:

A vision has to "reframe" the known scene, to reconceptualize the obvious, connect the previously unconnected dream.

Others may prefer the term mission, but rather than getting bogged

down in semantical discussion of vision and mission in this short introduction, both may be seen as goals that unite an organization and help
create a plan for the future that can inspire and put all staff members on
the same wavelength. Reading the listed books and articles will illustrate
more clearly the differences between vision and mission, as well as their
potential impact upon strategic planning.

27. Ackoff, Russell L. "Creating the Corporate Future: Plan or Be
    Planned For." New York: John Wiley & Sons, 1981.

28. Barkdoll, Gerald L. "Scoping Versus Coping: Developing a Com-
    prehensive Agency Vision." *Public Administration Review* 52 #4
    (July/August 1992): 330-338.

29. Beck, Robert N. "Visions, Values, and Strategies: Changing
    Attitudes and Culture." *Academy of Management Executive 1* #1
    (February 1987): 33-41.

30. Belasco, James A. "Teaching the Elephant to Dance." New York:
    Crown Publishers, 1990. [Chapter 6: Vision Makes the Difference]

31. Belasco, James A. "This Vision Thing." *Executive Excellence 7* #1
    (January 1990): 3-4.

32. Below, Patrick J. "The Executive Guide to Strategic Planning."
    San Francisco: Jossey-Bass, 1987.

33. Bryson, John, ed. "Strategic Planning for Public Service and
    Non-Profit Organizations." Tarrytown, NY: Pergamon Press, 1993.

34. Carr, David K. and Ian D. Littman. "Excellence in Government:
    Total Quality Management in the 1990s." [Chapter 8]
    Arlington, VA: Coopers & Lybrand, 1990.

35. Collins, James C. and Jerry I. Porras. "Organizational Vision and
    Visionary Organizations." *California Management Review 34* #1
    (Fall 1991): 30-52.

36. Digman, Lester. "Strategic Management: Concepts, Decisions, Cases." Plano, TX: Business Publications, Inc., 1986.

37. Halachmi, Arie. "Strategic Planning and Management? Not Necessarily." *Public Productivity Review* No.40 (Winter 1986): 35-50.

38. Handbook of Strategic Planning. New York: J. Wiley, 1986.

39. Handy, Charles. "The Age of Unreason." Boston: Harvard Business School Press, 1989. [see especially p. 134-136 "The Language of Leadership."]

40. Kaufman, Roger. "Strategic Planning Plus." Beverly Hills, CA: Sage Publications, 1992.

41. Langeler, Gerard H. "The Vision Trap." *Harvard Business Review 70* #2 (March-April 1992): 46-50, 52-55.

42. Mainelli, Michael. "Vision into Action: A Study of Corporate Culture." *Journal of Strategic Change* 1 (1992): 189-201.

43. Melcher, Bonita H. "Strategic Planning: Development and Implementation." Blue Ridge Summit, PA: TAB Books, 1988.

44. Nanus, Burt. "Visionary Leadership: How to Re-Vision the Future." *Futurist 26* #5 (September/October 1992): 20-25.

45. NASA. Vision Team Final Report. Washington, D.C.: NASA, 1993.

46. Quigley, Joseph V. "Vision: How Leaders Develop It, Share It, and Sustain It." New York: McGraw-Hill, 1992.

47. Senge, Peter. "The Fifth Discipline." New York: Doubleday, 1990. [Chapter 11: Shared Vision]

48. Stace, Doug A. and Dexter C. Dunphy. "Translating Business Strategies into Action: Managing Strategic Change." *Journal of Strategic Change 1* #4 (July-August 1992): 203-216.

49. "Strategic Planning for Action and Results." New York: Conference Board, 1991.

24 • PLACE AND FUNCTIONALITY OF REFERENCE SERVICES

FROM THE PERSPECTIVE OF TOTAL QUALITY MANAGEMENT THEORY

Alfred Willis and Eugene E. Matysek, Jr.

Theoretically, the quantity of reference services provided by a library may be regarded as an index of the inefficiency with which the library is operating. At the same time, the provision of reference services can arguably perpetuate existing inefficiencies in the library's operation and even exacerbate them.

In any library, the general process to be carried on is that of putting specific, concrete embodiments of informative material ("information packets," such as books, journals, sound recordings, maps, microfilms, output from machine-readable data files, etc.) into the hands of individual patrons in response to particular queries.

In a library operating under a self-help paradigm, patrons define their queries for themselves and answer these queries by locating first the library, then the optimally relevant information packets available in or through that library. In libraries operating under a patron-assisted paradigm, patrons request specific information packets which are then retrieved by their surrogates on the library staff (*e.g.*, pages). One oath other of these paradigms (or perhaps some combination of both of them) provides the organizational model for virtually all modern American academic and public libraries. In either case, patron satisfaction is a function of the degree to which the general library process operates effectively.

Alfred Willis, currently Head of the Arts Library, University of California, Los Angeles, was formerly Architecture Librarian, Kent State University.

Eugene E. Matysek, Jr. (1950-1993) was an Operations Research Analyst and Special Assistant for Total Quality Management, Defense Fuel Supply Center, Cameron Station, Alexandria, Virginia

This article originally appeared in the electronic journal *LIBRES*, vol. 2 no. 8, August, 1992 and was distributed by e-mail to registrants before each of the Institutes as part of their reading assignment. It is reprinted here with permission of the authors.

Any process can be described as a series of events progressively moving forward over time to produce products or services for a customer. The principal elements of the general library process are easily identified. The customers of this process are the patrons of the library. The inputs to the process are acquired, cataloged, and properly stored information packets whose topics cover a determined area of human knowledge. The outputs of the process are the information packets a library's customers retrieve or receive on various occasions in response to their queries. Library management undertakes the task of producing access to these packets, i.e., of assuring the ongoing movement of information packets through a library's physical space to its customers at optimal rates of both effectiveness and efficiency. This task is complex, and typically involves a labor force divided into several departmental contingents, one of which commonly consists of a cadre of more or less full-time reference librarians.

In contemporary American academic and public libraries, the need for reference librarians is almost always taken for granted. An analysis of the general library process would suggest, however, that far from being a necessary component of such a process functioning at optimal efficiency, much if not all reference service actually functions as a corrective for occasional processual inefficiencies.

In an optimally functioning library, information packets are selected and acquired at optimal efficiency. It will therefore possess exactly the right books, journals, databases, etc., that patrons will require, and these items will be delivered to the library quickly (or otherwise supplied, as in the case of online services, without interruption). It will catalog the information packets it acquires quickly and accurately. These items will thus be correctly described in the library's records, they will receive correct and full subject analysis, and to each of their records all relevant descriptive and subject headings will be assigned. The optimally functioning library will maintain its catalog in such a way that it will be usable by patrons with a modicum of knowledge of its purpose and nature. The library will also take steps to teach the mastery of that knowledge. The library will store its information packets optimally (quickly and accurately), so that patrons will find each one in its proper place. The sympathetic positioning of correctly functioning equipment for accessing "disembodied information" (*e.g.*, CD-ROM players) is tantamount to storing more traditional information packets (*e.g.*, books) in proper order. All mobile information packets (i.e., internally or externally circulating items) will be returned to their proper places as quickly and accurately as possible after each displacement. Furthermore, in order to operate at all, the optimally functioning library's facility must be open, clearly arranged, free of cumbersome barriers, well lighted, and appropriately climate- controlled. Its electronic equipment will be maintained in good working order and kept functioning without unplanned interruptions....

In an optimally functioning library, a patron with a modicum of knowledge of its organizational scheme (or the patron's surrogate) should, without the assistance of a reference librarian and without undue delay, be able to retrieve or receive the most suitable information packets required to answer a given query.

But in real life, of course, patrons in self-help libraries are not able to retrieve exactly the right information packet responding to their queries in minimal time, every time. Instead, they experience more or less frequent failures of the library process. In patron-assisted libraries also, patrons experience similar failures. In such events, patrons are often encouraged to seek the assistance of reference librarians.

If a library failure is attributable to the library's failure to acquire the best source answering to a particular query, a reference librarian may be asked to suggest alternative sources. In so far as these sources are qualitatively inferior, harder to use, or more expensive to access (*e.g.*, via interlibrary loan), the reference librarian cannot actually correct the failure but can only mitigate its effects.

If a library failure is attributable to the library's failure to catalog the best source properly (*e.g.*, used incorrect cataloging copy without editing it to remove significant errors in headings) or quickly, the reference librarian might be asked to imagine alternate retrieval strategies (*e.g.*, through elaborate Boolean keyword searching of the catalog). Failing this, the reference librarian might suggest an alternative source.

If a library failure is attributable to the library's failure to store the best source in its proper place (*e.g.*, retained a shelver without adequate knowledge of the call-number system), again the reference librarian might be asked to suggest an alternative source.

In all such cases, reference work appears as a quality-control subprocess at the end of one or more failed library sub-processes. It occurs then in reaction to the consequences that the failed sub-process(es) have for patrons, i.e., unacceptable products of the library process as a whole.

Admittedly, libraries often invite their patrons to consult a reference librarian before a failure occurs. In that case (when a library's staff, management, and patrons have all come to expect failures in service as a matter of routine), reference service appears as a prophylactic rather than as a corrective.

But whether it operates before the fact or after the fact to reverse or mitigate the effects on a patron of an anticipated or actual library failure, in so far as it operates only on failed products of the general library process and not on the process itself, the work involved in reference service is of a nature entirely different from that of the value-adding work carried out in most other library departments. It is bibliographers, technical-services personnel, and document-delivery staff who assure the functioning of the really crucial sub-processes in a library. It is they who can contribute the basic, value-added functions of selection, acquisition, cataloging, shelving, final packaging, etc. Theirs are the sub-processes that cannot be eliminated without eliminating the library altogether; the sub-processes which do break down due to understaffing, poor equipment, lack of training, etc., hence causing the problems for patrons that reference librarians typically try to solve, but whose efficiencies library management must be concerned with optimizing.

One obstacle to the optimization of sub-processual efficiency in any system, including libraries, is the scarcity of fiscal resources available for investment in strategic improvement in one or another value-adding sub-process. The significance of this obstacle is exacerbated to the extent that organizations spend any proportion of their resources on value-reducing efforts—however effective they may be—to correct quality flaws found in their products.

Quality-control processes are inherently costly. They comprise reactions to problems rather than constructive improvements to failing or failed processes. Because quality-control processes are therefore the least cost-effective components of any system, eliminating them holds the greatest promise for reducing system costs. Conversely, investing in improvements to the value-adding sub-processes of a system holds the greatest promise for its functional amelioration.

In a library, optimizing the value-adding sub-processes of acquisitions, cataloging, facilities maintenance, etc., obviously should minimize the need for the quality control typically provided by reference services.

Although increasing investment in a library's administrative and technical sub-processes thus clearly holds the greatest promise both for enhancing its effectiveness and for reducing its costs by reducing the likelihood or incidence of processual failures, increasing investment in reference services is generally easier to justify. Increasing investment in reference services is especially easy to justify in a library already functioning sub-optimally, where the sub-optimal functioning itself will generate in the patron population a constant demand for corrective reference assistance. The justification will quite literally materialize itself, in the bodies of patrons who, having experienced library failures, line up in growing numbers before the reference desk to request assistance. Strictly speaking, it is the number of such patrons that is the index of a library's processual inefficiency. But in so far as a library commits fiscal and human resources to reference services in the expectation that those services could make up in effectiveness what was lost to patrons through inefficiency, the quantity of reference services provided becomes, by extension and proportionally, itself the index.

The danger for library management in accepting uncritically any proposed justification for continued or even increased reference services, however, is considerable—especially in those libraries operating with finite human resources (i.e., all libraries?) and consequently forced to finance the proposed quality-control efforts out of savings in those departments charged with the execution of the inherently value-adding sub-processes. In such a case, increasing investment in reference services would be expected to lead to increasing degradation of the general library process, and ultimately to the total collapse of the library system.

SOME PERTINENT LITERATURE

Crosby, Philip B. Quality is Free
New York: McGraw-Hill, 1983.

Deming, W. Edwards. Out of the Crisis
Cambridge, MA: MIT Center for Advanced Engineering Study, 1982.

Taylor, Robert S. *Value-Added Processes in Information Systems*
Norwood, NJ: Ablex, 1986.

White, Herbert S. "The Value-Added Process of Librarianship."
Library Journal 114 (January 1989): 62-63.

Wormell, Irene, ed. *Information Quality: Definitions and Dimensions*
London: Taylor Graham, 1990.

25 • A REPLY TO WILLIS AND MATYSEK

Charles A. Bunge

School of Library and Information Studies
University of Wisconsin Madison, February 25, 1993

Through the wonders of electronic mail, interactive communications be-
gan well before the Institute. Registrants received the Willis-Matysek
article a month prior to the Berkeley Institute; two weeks later they
received this response. —Editor

The Willis and Matysek article is very interesting. Surely, reference librarians and reference managers want their services to be value-adding services and to contribute to the optimal efficiency of their libraries. Willis and Matysek argue that reference services are merely quality-control processes that exist to make up for failures in other sub-processes of the library. If these services were operating optimally, there would be no need for reference services; and, indeed, the operation of reference services can take attention and resources from other (value-adding) sub-processes.

At the purely theoretical level their argument may be plausible. For their "optimally functioning library" this would seem to require at least the following: Complete knowledge of the information needs of the library's clientele, so that the appropriate (and only the appropriate) "information packets" will be selected and acquired; complete knowledge of how individual clients will conceptualize or formulate their information needs on entering the library system, so that information packets will be cataloged with the appropriate (and only the appropriate) access points; and a mechanism for assisting individual clients in moving their conceptions of their information need from vague feelings of need to conceptions with sufficient clarity and focus to be serviceable by the library's access system and by information packets.

In real life (to use Willis' and Matysek's term), we know that such complete knowledge of patron needs and thought processes is impossible. The collection builder and the cataloger must operate on what might be called hypothetical knowledge or knowledge based on probabilities. The thought process involved in collection building goes something like this: "From what I know of our clientele, including their past information needs and my best projections of their future information needs, I should acquire this item (or I should not acquire this item and let the system provide access rather than ownership)." For the cataloger, the thought process is something like" "From what I know of our clientele and their ways of conceptualizing their information needs, I should provide the following access points for this information packet." The same kind of thought process is involved for the expert system designer who attempts to design an interface between the conceptualizations of individual users and the various paths that can be used to get to relevant information packets.

In real life, lacking such complete knowledge, the natural tendency of the collection builder, the cataloger, and the system designer is to "hedge their bets" (i.e., attempt to increase the probability that relevant information packets will be owned and that they will be found) by acquiring as many information packets as possible, by applying as many access points as possible, and by anticipating every conceivable client quirk in the expert system interface. All of us know that such an approach can lead to great inefficiencies and waste of resources. But, given the state of our knowledge and ability to predict information needs and information-seeking behavior of library clients, it is very difficult to do otherwise with good precision.

Enter reference service. Reference service can be defined as personal assistance given to an individual (or small sub-group of the library's clientele) whose information need is known (or ascertained) at the time the service is provided. Rather than operating on hypothetical knowledge, this "sub-process" operates on actual knowledge of an actual information need of an actual client. The reference librarian and the client, acting collaboratively, can manipulate the access systems of the library (including bibliographic and other reference tools) to find information that is relevant to that actual information need. This service truly adds value to the information packets that have been acquired by getting them used and adds value to the cataloging by helping the client use it successfully.

Willis and Matysek are correct in characterizing reference service as a sub-system that helps users deal successfully with the results of decisions made by other sub-processes of the library. Because the collection developer, the cataloger, and the expert system designer know there is and will continue to be a reference service, they can decrease their tendency to over-buy, over-catalog, and over-design. Rather than view reference service as a compensating process that makes up for errors made by other sub-processes, we should view reference services as an important sub-process that should work in harmony and cooperation with the other sub-processes. The real optimization to be sought in a library is optimum balance between the work done at the "input" level (i.e., the level where the knowledge of information needs and information seeking behavior is hypothetical and incomplete) and that done at the "output" level (i.e., when a real client presents a real information need to the system). Obviously, if too few information packets are acquired and too few access points are provided, even excellent reference service cannot get clients to the information they need. Obviously as well (to me at least), if high quality reference service is not available, resources acquired and cataloged will not serve client needs optimally.

It is my view that, no matter how much our ability to provide immediate and real-time physical access to information increases, no matter how much our ability to provide detailed and complete bibliographic and index access to information increases, information systems that are designed to operate without the need for human-to-human interactions (i.e., reference services) will collapse under their own weight and complexity (at least those designed for large, heterogeneous clienteles). Libraries that are designed to take full advantage of technology; of our increasing knowledge of information sources, communication processes, and human information-seeking behavior; *and* of the reference librarian's ability to help clients clarify information needs and use information access systems effectively will be the true "optimally functioning" libraries of the future.

The Strategic Visions Steering Committee

Background: In mid-1991, a grassroots effort to create a strategic vision for librarianship for the 21st century took hold. Stimulated by wide-ranging discussion on two listservs, about 85 people met at the June 1991 meeting of the American Library Association. It was felt that in responding on the one hand to crises such as the closing of library schools, a perceived lack of leadership, and budgetary reductions, and on the other hand to the wonderful opportunities afforded by technological developments to provide new services, librarians in all sectors will need to come together to formulate their vision and strategic direction. Subsequently, the Strategic Visions Steering Committee (SVSC) was formed—funded primarily by the Council on Library Resources, and comprised of leaders from all segments of the library and information profession—to pinpoint critical issues facing the profession and to move the profession as a whole in new directions. Since SVSC first issued its "Visions" and "Values" documents in early 1992, representatives of SVSC have held "visions" discussions with countless professional groups throughout the United States and established a "visions" Internet conference.

To subscribe to the conference, address your message to:

listserv@library.sdsu.edu

Your message should then read:

Subscribe Visions <Your Name>
(*Example*: Subscribe Visions Jane Doe)

To send a message to the subscriber list, address your message to:

visions@library.sdsu.edu

Below are the *draft* statements of "vision" and "values" generated by the Strategic Vision Steering Committee at its meeting at Georgetown University in early December 1991. This document reflects the group's response to PACS-L and LIBADMIN input, as well as the discussion at the Strategic Visions Discussion Group meeting prior to ALA in Atlanta in June 1991. Taken into consideration were concerns about the strategic direction of the profession, and the widespread desire to develop a discussion document to be made available to all members of the profession. The anticipation is that further discussion in open forums will allow refinement of the statement, as well as a mutual agreement and understanding of the vision of the librarian and librarianship of the future.

STRATEGIC VISION FOR PROFESSIONAL LIBRARIANS

Establish the basis for librarianship in the 21st century in:

SERVICE

- By selecting and delivering information that users need at the point and moment of need
- By creating and maintaining systems which provide accurate and reliable information
- By promoting the design of information systems that require little or no learning time for effective use
- By correctly analyzing users' questions and providing them with the information they need (which may not be reflected accurately in their questions)
- By educating users to manage information
- By initiating contact with potential information seekers to ensure a widespread understanding of professional services available to them, including assistance for those who do not wish to use the library independently
- By furthering the development of the "virtual library," a concept of information housed electronically and deliverable without regard to its location or to time

LEADERSHIP

- By taking responsibility for information policy development, information technology application, environmental awareness, information research, and risk-taking in making strategic choices in the information arena
- By accepting accountability for the information services we provide
- By identifying and collaborating with strategic partners and allies in information delivery

INNOVATION

- By experimenting with new forms of organizational structure and staffing within libraries to enable delivery of new types of services to users, especially remote users, or users of the growing "virtual library"
- By recognizing and supporting the library without walls, and the capacity of library services to be provided in various environments

RECRUITMENT/DEVELOPMENT

- By publicizing the unique advantage at which the "information age" places librarians as information professionals
- By strengthening the degree-granting programs, developing effective relationships with other information-related disciplines, and establishing alternative models for attaining professional credentials
- By attracting and retaining creative and innovative people
- By incorporating different competencies/professionals into the emerging information delivery environment
- By addressing the importance of continuing professional education

VALUES AND QUALITIES OF LIBRARIANSHIP: DISCUSSION DRAFT

At the December 1991 meeting of the Strategic Visions Steering Committee, the group was asked to address the question of those personal professional values that should be stressed and that should accompany a profession-wide strategic vision statement. While it was generally agreed that a values statement was desirable, it became evident that it was the most difficult task that the group set for itself. Several issues were prominent in their lack of resolution and their apparent need for further discussion:

Issue #1: the distinction between the values of libraries as institutions and the values of librarians as professionals was not easy to make. As a result, for example, some urged that values such as "freedom of access to information" should be stated, while others argued that this was more of an institutional value, and suggested values such as "commitment to the profession," or "tolerance of diversity of opinions."

Issue #2: in addressing the qualities that were thought to be desirable for librarians of the future, some suggested that these are qualities that are either obvious, or that are so general that they are qualities desirable for all professions and are not unique to librarianship. Further discussion has suggested that even if the qualities are obvious, and even if they are not unique to librarianship, perhaps we should state them and underscore them so that people entering the profession, evaluating the profession, or recruiting to library schools, will understand that the profession wants the best and brightest, and has high expectations of its members.

Issue #3: an issue that was not discussed in depth but that might be closely linked to a values statement is the degree to which library schools and libraries attempt to recruit to the profession people who have the qualities and share the values that we indicate are appropriate for the 21st century librarian.

This discussion document is in three parts:

1. the draft statement of values that emanated from the plenary discussion of the Strategic Vision Steering Committee

2. value statements that were identified in small group discussion prior to that plenary session, but that were not included in the plenary document

3. a list of qualities that we as librarians already seem to emphasize, based on advertisements for professional positions.

It is hoped that groups discussing the vision statement will also be able to look carefully at the values/qualities issue, and make suggestions and comments on both documents.

I. Draft Statement of Values

In a democratic society, information is power and leads to knowledge. The librarian facilitates access to information by ensuring:
- preservation of recorded information
- organization of information to enable retrieval
- equal opportunity for access to information, and
- a climate that fosters/promotes/invites use.

In facilitating access, we value:
- privacy
- confidentiality
- intellectual freedom
- users' ability to find information independently
- initiating awareness in the community of the librarian's role and
  services provided
- literacy
- continuing professional development

II. Values identified by small group discussions

We value:
- tolerance of diversity of opinions
- professional leadership through innovation, quality service and
  partnerships
- cooperation/sharing/networking
- innovation and risk-taking
- collaborative services involving clients; other organizations; other
  professions; other members of the information professions
- client-driven orientation
- commitment to the profession
- flexibility to consider new ideas and change in the workplace
- curiosity
- analytical reasoning

III. Individual qualities that may be appropriate for inclusion in a values
statement

We may have, as a profession, some qualities or traits that we consider "valuable" in librarians. If this is true, then we should be recruiting

people who appear to possess these same traits into the profession (i.e. into our master's programs). Is there any way that we might want to incorporate these traits, or a subset thereof, into our values statement? The qualities listed below are related to the individual, and not to the experience that the individual may gain during his or her life. These are some of them, quoted directly from our own job ads:

Interpersonal and communication skills
Ability to adapt; flexibility
Vision
Leadership skills or potential
Commitment to professional staff development
Commitment to a service orientation; to providing quality service
Commitment to a highly productive work environment
Ability to function as a member of a team; to work collaboratively
Understanding of the internal and external environment
Potential for scholarly and professional achievement
Innovation, energy, enthusiasm, creativity, professionalism, initiative
Articulate spokesperson for the library; public relations talents
Ability to organize and relate to a diverse staff
Ability to work effectively, both independently and cooperatively
Ability to produce results in a persuasive and timely manner
Good judgment, candor, sense of proportion and the practical
Commitment to excellence

18 January 1992

27 • 21ST CENTURY JOB DESCRIPTION

Anne G. Lipow
Director, Library Solutions Institute

The message below was posted on the Internet to the Visions network discussion group in early August 1992.

Wishing to contribute to the creation of job models we'd like to strive for, the Strategic Visions Steering Committee assigned me the task of drafting a hypothetical job ad for a future librarian position. Below is the result. It is futuristic in the sense that libraries are not organized in the way implied by the job description, and no one that I know of currently has such a job. However, it is entirely realistic: the technology on which it draws is feasible today, and the basic mission of this future librarian is much the same as it is today. I hoped that this 21st century librarian would be very recognizable to us and that the job would seem to us utterly doable. Which is why I picked a not-too-distant year for the ad. As you can tell, I had fun thinking about it. I'd be interested in responses.

—Anne Lipow

LIBRARY POSITION ANNOUNCEMENT

February 2020

Historical context

1. THE TELEDESK

What we know today as the teledesk—which is still evolving, primarily to include more international connections—originated in the final decade of last century. Before 1994, clients had to go to a "reference desk," situated within each separate library location where actual-collections, no matter how small, were housed. The reference desk was the primary means of dispensing consulting services. Obviously, this location-dependent service was too remote to reach any but a small proportion of potential clients, and too costly to maintain. The "reference librarians," as they were called, who staffed the desk, used primarily the resources physically at hand to answer the questions asked by the walk-in traffic!

The idea of the teledesk was inspired by a restaurant reservation service that had been operating at DisneyWorld for many years, and looked essentially like this: the reservations seeker approached one of many service counters located throughout the park. On the other side of the counter was attached a giant TV screen, and when the client pressed a "Start here" button, a life-size friendly person appeared on the screen and conducted the interview, in quite the same manner as librarians did at the reference desk. That is, two-way cameras enabled each to see the other, and the scope of the screen enabled the client to see the staff person in action, read the selected restaurant menus, and receive all the important visual cues of an in-person service.

Today's teledesk includes innovations to its Disney predecessor, such as the ability to download information to either a printer or disk at the client station; and a call-back button for recalling the staff person who has "disappeared" to help others, leaving the client to manipulate and study material that the staff person displayed on the screen.

While many resisted the change to the remote service, charging that it would be impersonal and robot-like, the opposite proved to be true. Highly personable professionals, expert in dealing with a variety of personalities, cultural differences and surprise situations staff the desk. The only negative difference between the in-person service and the remote service was possibly that the staff person and client could not shake hands. However, around the turn of the century a practice arose that has become an international convention: staff and client "touch" forefingers on the screen—especially as a parting gesture. (A recent embellishment by some high school users of the public library teledesk may be spreading in popularity: a rather complicated "handshake" that involves a sequence of maneuvers using all fingers, the palm, the front and back of the wrist, and the elbow. Parents have begun to protest the inclusion of hip-action in this ritual.)

2. NECST AND NECST-IN-LINE

The National Educational Cooperative of Stratified Teleservices, NECST, is, as everyone knows, the government agency that coordinates cooperative advisory services, cooperative resource building and sharing, and cooperative cataloging and indexing. In cooperative advisory services, member libraries offer a designated level of service to all citizenry via the teledesk: FIRST LEVEL (generalist service), RESEARCH LEVEL (staffed by specialists), and THAUMATURGICAL LEVEL (by referral only)—depending on the expertise and training of the professional, as well as on the actual and virtual information resources at hand. Though NECST is now taken for granted, it was slow to gain acceptance. Not until the establishment of NECST-IN-LINE (which routes your local caller to the next available consultant in the country when your library's consultants are busy with clients) did the remote "reference desk" take hold in public and academic libraries throughout the country. Cooperative advisory service was now mainstreamed (as had been interlibrary cooperation a decade before when GLOBENET opened the way for ILL to be mainstreamed). Just as the embryonic versions of GLOBENET (ARPANet, Internet, NREN, etc.) promoted a widespread understanding that access to information need not be dependent either on where the information resides nor on where the searcher is located, so too it was now realized that consulting services (or, as they called it in the old days, "reference service") need not be dependent on both the service provider and the service recipient being in the same place.

3. CONTACT HOURS

In the discharge of "contact hour" duties, Advisory Service Consultants (ASCs) are expected to work with clients in a partnership relationship. That is, unlike their forerunner "reference librarians," whose primary relationship with clients emanated from their introductory question "How can I help?", the ASC provides what the client needs primarily through listening. By being present (physically or virtually) at their clients' meetings, colloquia, etc.; reading their research proposals; belonging to their organizations and discussion groups; being on the same mailing lists as their clients; etc., the ASC learns what resources would help and provides the information needed; introduces the client(s) to appropriate resources unfamiliar to them, and, if necessary, teaches the client(s) how to use those resources; and even produces, or arranges to be produced a needed resource that doesn't yet exist.

4. A CHANGE IN PHILOSOPHY AND FOCUS

Sometime in the mid-1990's the librarian's philosophy shifted from expecting users to learn the library to expecting the library to learn the user.

POSITION AVAILABLE

Library Consultant: Humanities specialist
Halcyon University Library, Research & Information Advisory Service

The Library of Halcyon University supports the research, instructional, and information needs of its 8,000 faculty, students and staff; and is a Research Level participant in NECST. This position is central to fulfilling the library's mission to provide instructional and consultation services to the local, regional, and national humanities research communities, and to construct and select research and information resources appropriate to the changing needs of the campus constituencies.

RESPONSIBILITIES:

Teledesk duties:

Serve an average of 8 hours a week on the Library teledesk, answering questions transmitted through library information stations located throughout the campus, including branch libraries, faculty and administrative offices, and dormitories.

Also serve 2 hours a week on the NECST network, providing advisory service to the national research communities in the humanities. (Halcyon also subscribes to the NECST-IN-LINE humanities service, which provides back-up advisory services.)

Contact duties:

ASCs are required to meet a standard of 40 contact-hours per month, 20 hours of which should be working with individuals or small classroom or research groups on their projects; and the balance in providing information services to targeted campus groups through producing an electronic news bulletin, participating in faculty networked discussion groups, and conducting classes for faculty, students, and staff in information resources in the humanities.

Resources development: Approximately one-quarter time is spent in selecting appropriate materials for actual-and virtual-collections in the humanities, as well as working with systems developers, telecommunications personnel, and other information professionals to design and construct humanities databases and multimedia systems that require no learning time.

Professional development: Keep abreast of new developments in user needs; trends in storage, retrieval, conservation, and delivery of information resources; and principles of systems design. To this end, ASCs are expected to spend up to one-quarter time maintaining active contact with colleagues and other informational professionals through electronic discussion groups, attendance at conferences, performing research and sharing the results, and learning new skills in preparation for taking on responsibilities in program planning and management.

QUALIFICATIONS:

Advanced degree in Librarianship required, with a specialization in user-agent systems preferred; depth of knowledge about resources and contemporary research issues in the humanities. Energy, enthusiasm for solving client's informational problems, and ability to thrive in conditions of ambiguity and rapid change. Skilled in question handling and instructional techniques. Demonstrated knowledge of applications of current and emerging technology as it contributes to meeting the needs of researchers in the humanities. Ability to plan, design, and evaluate library networking systems; ability to communicate clearly, knowledgeably, and personably, orally and in writing, with a variety of client constituencies and colleagues. Demonstrated ability to work both independently and as part of a team.

SALARY:

Comparable to entry-level compensation in other service professions such as medicine and law.

28 • REORGANIZATION IN REFERENCE DEPARTMENTS

A SUMMARY OF SURVEY RESPONSES

Anne G. Lipow

This report was first posted to the electronic discussion lists LIBADMIN and LIBREF-L on January 6, 1992.

PREFACE

In early September 1991, I asked on LIBADMIN and LIBREF-L for descriptions of innovative reorganized reference services or redefined positions in reference departments. My reason for asking was to sketch out a few models of non-traditional organizational structures as a basis for discussion with reference staff in a couple of libraries that were rethinking their services. I certainly got the raw material for that limited purpose, but much more is there for more systematic analysis than I have the inclination to undertake. What follows is simply an amalgamation of the responses, with a few impressions tossed in.

THE RESPONDENTS

People from 20 libraries, all academic, responded—by personal e-mail, fax, U.S. Post Office, and telephone call. They were library directors, heads of reference departments, and staff, not necessarily from reference, who participated in reference change. Two explicitly asked to remain anonymous, and a few others implied by their candor that they assumed I would not identify specific people or libraries; so to be safe, with a few exceptions, I will not mention names.

IMPETUS FOR CHANGE

The responding reference departments are undertaking major changes—whether independently or as part of a total library reorganization—for one or more of the following reasons (some for all of them): (a) integrated automated library systems require improved communication and coordination among staff within reference departments as well as between technical service and public service staffs, and current/past organization seems to impede those processes; (b) improved and different services are required to meet patrons' new needs for delivery of information, and current/past organization and staffing seem unable to accommodate those requirements; (c) present/past staffing patterns are inadequate to meet patrons' need to be taught new searching concepts and how to use new tools; (d) with bibliographic information about other libraries' holdings so readily available to the end user, libraries must gear up for providing information and material wherever it exists and not try to own everything that their patrons need; (e) budget reductions, staff freezes, and grim fiscal outlook require reconsidering expectations and goals, and re-examining how business is done.

I found quite interesting that of those who included budget problems as a reason, many felt the changes were beneficial and probably should have been done regardless of budget. As one director put it, "Economics forced me to do what I wanted to do anyway." Or, as a department head noted, "Budget may have set the pace and magnitude of the changes, but it isn't responsible for the direction..." They seemed to be saying that it takes a crisis to get us to move!

GOALS AND STRATEGIES

Better service to the campus community was the priority goal that the respondents hoped to reach by reorganization. New services desired centered around instructional programs beyond BI; service points and functions based on CD ROM and other electronic information resources; and a more proactive approach to reference, especially calling for increased contact with faculty, initiating assistance by going to where the patron is, and for delivery of the information itself. In an abstract the author sent me of a paper she presented, Mara Pinckard (Arizona State University) wrote what others said in different ways or in different degrees: "...the user will continue to be more sophisticated in needs but not in 'access abilities' and we must respond with a revolution in academic reference services."

While several respondents drew a link between their goals and the structural changes they were making, I was not always able to comprehend that link. From this outsider's standpoint, some seemed to be simply renaming traditional services to convey a more accurate message to

208

the patron of the services offered, or regrouping units to gain efficiencies in providing existing services. Regrouping existing services under "Access Services" is an example. Though those respondents described that change as facilitating new goals, the functions that were subsumed under "Access" were not renamed, and they were different for each library, so it was hard for me to see the relationship between goal and structure. For example, one library's Access Services included BI, another didn't; one included ILL, another didn't. One library went in the other direction: it DISMANTLED its groupings and the now separate units (reference, circulation, acquisitions, etc.) all report to one Associate Director! This library's goal was improved service through a "less hierarchical style...The emphasis is now on interaction and cooperation between units, with conflicts mediated by the Associate Director or Director, as appropriate." I suspect that in most cases the breakthroughs accomplished by such reorganizations can be understood only in the context of local history. In some instances, the particular form of reorganization seemed to have more to do with what the administrator could work best with rather than based in a reassessment of the relationship between structure and services, even though that relationship was how the change was justified.

TYPES OF CHANGE

Some libraries had already undergone the changes they described, some had only a plan they were about to implement, and others were somewhere between the plan and completion. With some anomalies, the nature of the changes fell into four categories: (1) consolidating reference units and staff, or substantial rearrangements within a reference department, to achieve greater efficiencies and to enable the flexibility to provide new or improved services; (2) adding staff to reference services; (3) using the strengths of people differently without upsetting the existing organizational structure; and (4) redefining functions based on new concepts of mission and service, from which followed dramatic reorganization. Only one respondent confessed to cutting services strictly in reaction to budget stresses.

Three respondents whose libraries took different routes to change provided detailed information about their experiences: Karyle Butcher (Oregon State U.) told about consolidating reference points (read her and co-author Michael P. Kinch's insightful article in JAL, vol. 16, 1990, pp. 280-284—"Who calls the shots? The politics of Reference Reorganization"—analyzing the process and outcome of this change); Janet Crayne

(U. of Virginia) enumerated the pros and cons of dual appointments; and Chris Ferguson (U. of California at San Diego) renamed and reorganized his department internally. For all three, emphasis on the PROCESS of change was extremely important—at least as important as the outcome itself, and each had ideas and recommendations about how that process should look to go right.

In addition to dual assignments in technical services and reference, others whose goal was to add staff to public services did so by assigning non-MLS staff to technical services positions, including original cataloging, and reassigning or, as attrition allowed, reallocating the professional librarian positions to the reference department. And still others freed the time of reference librarians by creating a first-level information desk service staffed by non-MLS people, who referred as appropriate to the reference desk.

NEW CONCEPTS OF FUNCTION AND ORGANIZATION

My own imagination was particularly stimulated by a few respondents whose libraries were in one or another stage of undergoing change based on a new vision of the role of the library. Collectively, they used such phrases as "library without walls", "virtual library"; they downplayed ownership of collections for eventual need and raised to greater importance access to materials regardless of where located and delivery of information at the point of need; they looked forward to a greater partnership with faculty in the educational and research process; they saw increased decision-making taking place at the front lines and a concurrent need for flattening the current pyramidal organizational structure; they replaced the traditional organizational divisions of "public service" and "technical service" with new divisions. One saw the need to build new avenues of communication and cooperation among information owners, including libraries, and information producers to ensure the information remains at least somewhere. Another library is about to embark on a "refocusing on patron services" through a Total Quality Management (TQM) program of self-managing teams.

One library is considering reorganizing all departments under two umbrella divisions based on the complementary service concepts of intellectual access and physical access. Functions related to intellectual access include, among others, reference and cataloging; functions related to physical access include, among others, circulation and acquisitions. The "intellectual access" division would be called Information Access; the "physical access " division, Information Delivery. I'm not sure there's enough of a distinction in the sound of those divisions to convey their meaning, but I find their meaning to be quite exciting.

The most revolutionary of the concepts being implemented by respondents is taking place at U. of California at San Francisco Library which serves a medical school campus. There, a dual organization, headed by the University Librarian, who is also Assistant Vice Chancellor for Academic Information Management, is being established consisting of Information Resources and Services on the one hand, and Center for Knowledge Management on the other. University Librarian and author of the plan, Richard Lucier, explains the role of the Center for Knowledge Management this way: "Knowledge management is a model for scientific and scholarly communication in which faculty and research librarians share the responsibility for the collection, structuring, representation, dissemination and use of knowledge, using computing and communications technologies. What is remarkably different about the knowledge management role is that it insinuates the Library at the beginning of the information transfer cycle rather than at the end and focuses on information capture rather than access and use." The other division, Information Resources and Services, has responsibility for the more traditional library functions, including cataloging, which is done entirely by non-MLS staff, collection development, preservation, acquisitions, ILL, BI, "public service," and special collections.

In a less ambitious change, another library is appointing existing staff part time to new positions in line with desired service changes (data archivist, microcomputer specialist, multicultural service specialist), but those positions are seen as outside of reference, leaving "reference" to become a static service that equates only with working at the desk. In fact, in all the descriptions of adding new services outside traditional boundaries while leaving those traditional boundaries in place, I got the impression that at least from the director's standpoint, it was judged to be easier on everyone to leave the old structure in place so that traditional work could be continued by those who seemed to resist change, and to erect new structures around them that would handle innovation. The implied expectation was that eventually the old structure would wither away.

STRESS AND CHANGE

It is clear that change takes time and doesn't come without some degree of stress on the players. On the one hand, staff is pushed to change by already escalated stressful conditions; and on the other hand, the transition to a new order seems inevitably to cause more stress, even where there is general acceptance that the change is for the better. Several respondents mentioned stress in one way or another. From a director who consolidated functions so that now "everyone does everything": "People don't want to be thought of as generalists, so they resist consolidation and diversification." Despite the acknowledged benefits that outweigh the disadvantages, taking on new work, as happens in consolidation or dual assignments has many built-in stressor conditions. Split assignments, observed one respondent, "means doubled meetings, doubled paperwork, two sets of internal policies, two sets of busy and slow times, and, in certain cases, absorption of tension between 2 conflicting departments...Working half-time at a new job, in a department of low staffing, is taxing...."

One respondent described reference work today as much more complex than in earlier days: "...a typical reference librarian in this library 4 years ago did little else besides work at the reference desk. No one went to conferences, did projects or research. They did 20 hours a week at the desk. The newer hires have a second assignment, are attending meetings, joining committees, etc., but only doing 12 hrs/week at the desk. And yet the 12 hours seem like a burden. The desk work is getting harder in terms of numbers of questions and the nature of the questions; online systems complicate things a lot. In addition to desk time, we do online searching. We keep up with e-mail...For every body we have, we get fewer desk hours and less slack when someone is sick. We all say we like the desk work—after all, we are reference librarians—but it kills us. We look like we're coming off a swing shift at a factory and getting folks to take extra hours is hard." There is widespread acknowledgement that change is hard on those who don't want it to happen. But one respondent touched on frustrations felt by those who want to move with change but must cope with those who drag their feet: "...there have been attempts to drop or greatly de-emphasize some services here..., including...[maintaining a] vertical file, and compilation of subject bibliographies. No one, however, ever decisively said to drop these functions, so the people involved (who don't want to let go of them) still spend about as much time on them as they ever did. (You may be able to tell that this is a sore point with me.) All the reference librarians are considered responsible for knowing about electronic information sources, but some embrace them with much more enthusiasm than others..."

THE ACADEMIC LIBRARY OF THE FUTURE
A YEAR 2010 DRAFT PLAN FOR THE DUKE UNIVERSITY LIBRARIES

Ken Berger and Rich Hines

Perkins Library Reference Deartment
Duke University, Durham, North Carolina

INTRODUCTION

In early 1992 we had the opportunity to read a preliminary draft of Jerry Campbell's article, "Shaking the Conceptual Foundations of Reference: A Perspective" (which ultimately appeared in the Winter 1992 issue of Reference Services Review). In that essay Dr. Campbell proposed that academic libraries devote three percent of their budgets to R&D. How would this money be spent? What direction should such an effort take? In an effort answer these and other questions the two of us brainstormed three issues: what the library/information access environment would be like in 2010; what the present environment is like in relation to that projected future; and what we in the academic library profession can do to be participants in this process. The written consolidation of our sessions was the discussion paper entitled "The Academic Library of the Future: A Year 2010 Draft Plan for the Duke University Libraries."

We shared the paper with Dr. Campbell, as well as other members of the Perkins Library staff. The intention was to stimulate and focus discussion of possible directions for future library planning. Such discussions have occurred, both within the library and at other forums at Duke and outside the university.

During these discussions Dr. Campbell stressed one point in particular: the importance of determining library user needs in planning for the future. Too many times library planning has been based upon inadequate understanding of our patrons' needs, and to a large extent we have forced users to conform to structures we have created and imposed upon their information seeking activities. New technologies and commercial ventures are making it possible for people to bypass the library in these activities, and if we are to have a role in the future it must be because we have a product people want, packaged in a way they find attractive and useful. With the assistance of a consumer research firm, PG Research Inc. of Raleigh, N.C., we are in the process of completing a market research project, which includes focus group interviews and a survey instrument sent to about five thousand members (faculty, students and staff) of the Duke University community. The goal was to achieve a better understanding of what our users really want. We intend to publish an article based on the survey results after the presentation of the final report by PG Research Inc.

PART ONE: WHERE WE WILL BE IN 2010

I. THE ACADEMIC LIBRARY IN 2010

1. Users seldom come into the library building; if they do, it will be for:
   - assistance with special problems
   - casual/recreational reading (primarily in paper format)
   - access to special equipment
   - access for those who lack appropriate equipment and/or expertise
   - contact with people
   - study hall
   - functions (e.g., wine and cheese parties)
   - instruction, group and individual (though some will be done via remote access or off-site visits)

2. Nearly all serials will appear in digitized format (all will probably be produced using computer technology)

3. A high-percentage of monographs will appear in digitized form, though much casual/recreational reading will still appear in paper format

4. Networking (the) standard
   - remote electronic access to a wide variety of formats and information through networks will be the norm; the market will force a high degree of standardization

5. CD-ROMS will have passed away as networking provides the primary distributed access to large databases and text files

- CD-ROMs may have a niche as access to information for who may need a portable information resource (who may customize disks for specific needs while not able to access networks)

6. Full text retrieval will be at least as standard as retrieval of bibliographic information is today

7. Library staffing way down as labor intensive aspects of the library institution decrease (section on "Functions of the Academic Librarian 2010" for more on this point)

8. Front end systems for accessing databases will be much more intuitive, greatly reducing the need for information intermediaries

9. Individual access to high quality computer equipment—screens which facilitate easy reading and the use of varied media—a given for every member of the university community

10. Library acquisition, personnel and maintenance costs way down

11. Library out of direct charge loop for access to databases and information services
    - users will have their own accounts
    - university/library will serve as brokers to obtain special rates with information services

12. Library and librarians will serve gateway role and as facilitators to those who need special assistance and/or access to esoteric materials

13. Library will continue to serve as an archive/museum for special materials (e.g., manuscripts, rare books, primary source items)

14. Memory/storage capabilities dramatically up; costs equally reduced

15. Large percentage of library holdings converted to digitized form

16. Advanced technologies and techniques (e.g., cluster and vector analysis) are used to index materials, providing the capability to search efficiently and successfully through the large databases which will be available

17. There will be new licensing and use fee structures, which will be reflective of the larger user base and lower-cost per use
    - assessments will be more directly tied to the information user

II. THE ACADEMIC LIBRARY USER IN 2010

1. Will have easy access to high quality computer equipment

2. Will have ready access to information networks

3. Will expect to be able to access computerized information systems with minimal instruction

4. Will expect to have access to all required readings online

5. Will expect to have access to all relevant reference materials online

6. Will expect to have access to most other materials, in most formats, online

7. Will not expect to have to enter library building or require librarian assistance, except for:
    *   access to special/esoteric materials
    *   some training
    *   information counseling
    *   assistance with difficult questions

8. Will accept assumption of use costs for information access comparable to present support of library activities (as built into cost of attending the university)

III. FUNCTIONS OF THE ACADEMIC LIBRARIAN IN 2010

1. Facilitators/PIGs (Professional/Personal Information Guides/ Gurus)
    *   training users
    *   providing access to esoteric materials
    *   information (technical/reference) counseling
    *   seeking out new information resources, and keeping users aware of them (though this may be a transparent operation)

2. Market Analysts
    *   surveying users to determine their needs and how well we meet those needs

3. Brokers
    *   negotiating access to information resources, equipment and lower costs

216

4. Conservators
   - identifying materials for conversion to machine-readable format

5. Researchers and Designers (R&D)
   - evaluating and improving existing systems and services, and development new resource capabilities

6. Reference
   - providing answers to difficult questions (Note: difficulty lies in the eyes of the requester)

7. Archivists
   - collecting, organizing and providing access to primary source and special materials (e.g., manuscripts and rare books) which may not be appropriately preserved and accessed only in digital form

8. Developers/Producers
   - assembling and creating new information resources and data bases, most likely from unique, local resources, for addition to the local/regional/national/international databases accessible through networks

PART TWO: WHERE WE ARE NOW
(IN RELATION TO WHERE WE WANT TO GO)

I. THE ACADEMIC LIBRARY IN 1992

1. "People will seldom come into the library . . ."

   Not true for those who have information needs; however there is presently little networking. Users do take advantage of telephone reference; Infoline (The Reference Department's bulletin board service which enables people with computers and modems to leave questions, make interlibrary loan requests, check library hours, etc.); dial in access to BIS (the online catalog); and ask for access to CD-ROMs remotely. Several have KI (Knowledge Index—a low cost, end user bibliographic searching service offered by Dialog) accounts. Many people (especially faculty) are already into networks. Many people use library primarily for reserve readings, study hall, light research (we believe)—many of their information needs need not be handled by presence in the building.

2. "Nearly all serials will appear in digitized format (all will probably be produced using computer technology)"

   We are experiencing the infancy of the electronic journal phenomenon now. Note also access to full-text through online search services such as Dialog and Lexis/Nexis; there are least hundreds, maybe thousands of journals available now (e.g., MacIntosh Libraries, an annual compilation of articles on the use of MacIntosh computers in libraries). Current access is primarily through Reference mediation and provision.

3. "A high-percentage of monographs will appear in digitized form, though much casual/recreational reading will still appear in paper format"

   Some are already available. For example: the Bible, the works of Shakespeare, the complete Sherlock Holmes, and the Library of the Future (hundreds of works of literature). As with journals, many more are being produced in electronic form, so the databases are being created.

4. "Networking (the) standard—remote electronic access to a wide variety of formats and information through networks will be the norm; the market will force a high degree of standardization"

   Look at all the Bitnet addresses in the Duke phone directory. Look at the library's LAN (local area network) and the university's network (Dukenet). Look at the existence of CompuServe, Genie, America Online, Prodigy, KI, Dialmail, BRS AfterDark—all aimed at the casual, non-professional searcher and user, as well as the more sophisticated audience. And the proliferation of e-mail and electronic bulletin board services. Standardization is not nearly there, but participation is already widespread.

5. "CD-ROMS will have passed away as networking provides the primary distributed access to large databases and text files . . . "

   CD-ROMs provide distributed access to databases and text that will be increasingly provided by networking. It will be much more cost effective to log into a particular database at point of need than to build up an extensive, expensive collection of CD-ROMs—which cannot be updated as frequently.

6. "Full text retrieval will be at least as standard as retrieval of bibliographic information is today"

   See #2 and #3 for new access to serials and monographs in full text. Users already want not just the citation—they want the document. It is even today sometimes cheaper to occasionally download an article than to regularly subscribe to the journal. (There is no analysis of this.) In any case, the desire is there.

7. "Library staffing way down as labor intensive aspects of the library . . . decrease . . ."

   Staffing still at relatively high level reflecting human intensive as pects of acquiring, processing, preserving and providing access to materials.

8. "Front end systems for accessing databases will be much more intuitive, greatly reducing the need for information intermediaries"

   Presently there is virtually no standardization across formats and platforms. We currently have formats for OCLC, Innovacq, Dialog and other online systems, a variety of CD-ROM systems, etc. There has been some standardization within product lines, e.g., Dialog and Silver Platter each present a variety of databases with the same search interface. But standardization is still in its infancy. Intuitive (i.e., user friendly) systems have been partially developed. They will get better as we improve use studies and artificial intelligence (AI); there is much potential for library input.

9. "Individual access to high quality computer equipment—which facilitate easy reading and use of varied media—a given for every member of the university community"

   Increasingly the case and an assumption of the university's plan. But there are still many library users (and staff!) who do not have access to equipment which makes reasonable use and access to existing and developing computerized information resources a possibility.

10. "Library acquisition, personnel and maintenance costs way down"

    Acquisition and personnel costs continue to rise dramatically; a reflection of our mode of maintaining current services and availability of resources while costs make this impossible.

11. "Library out of direct charge loop for access to databases and information services . . ."

Library currently absorbs costs of materials, processing and most computer retrieval (CD-ROM and online). Very few costs (other than as part of university budget) are passed on to users.

12. "Library and librarians will serve gateway role and as facilitators to those who need special assistance and/or access to esoteric materials"

   Already extensively involved as facilitator for users: teaching old and new library use techniques; finding answers to questions; locating and obtaining esoteric materials. All very labor intensive.

13. "Library will continue to serve as an archive/museum for special materials (e.g., manuscripts, rare books, primary source items)"

   We do this very well already.

14. "Memory/storage capabilities dramatically up; costs equally reduced"

   Already the case. Storage capabilities (especially CD-ROMs) make possible entire books on disk. A gigabyte of storage is not impossible, where 128K was a lot ten years ago. And there is the Rolls Royce analogy (if automotive technology had kept pace with microcomputer technology, the car would cost $25 and get 100 mph!).

15. "Large percentage of library holdings converted to digitized form"

   See #2 and #3 above. Still a minute percentage.

16. "Advanced technologies and techniques . . . are used to index materials, providing the capability to search efficiently and successfully through the large databases which will be available"

   Full text access opens up possibilities for retrieving information, but it is slow and inefficient (i.e., brings up too many false hits). True efficiency in this regard not yet here.

17. "There will be new licensing and use fee structures . . . reflective of the larger user base and lower-cost per use . . . assessments will be more directly tied to the information user"

   Copyright a big problem. Even some databases permit location and retrieval, but not use of the material. There are some document delivery services (CARL, Dialorder, ISI, etc.) which build copyright fees into service. Obviously an area of potential. We are currently absorbing most costs of computer searching (CD-ROM and online), but users have been also accepting more (e.g., KI and CompuServe).

II. THE ACADEMIC LIBRARY USER IN 1992

1. "Will have easy access to high quality computer equipment"

   Some have access to computer equipment, not much of it of high quality.

2. "Will have ready access to information networks"

   Some have access to networked systems, e.g., Dukenet, Bitnet/Internet, CompuServe, etc.; but we have a long way to go.

3. "Will expect to be able to access computerized information systems with minimal instruction"

   For the most part users manage some level of command of systems, but many need instruction beyond online help, and most are not using systems with much efficiency.

4. "Will expect to have access to all required readings online"

   This is just now being investigated—no expectation at present, though this service would be well received.

5. "Will expect to have access to all relevant reference materials online"

   Parallels #4.

6. "Will expect to have access to most other materials, in most formats, online"

   Parallels #4.

7. "Will not [normally] expect to have to enter library building or require librarian assistance . . ."

   We handle all the special situations now: "access to special/esoteric materials," "some training," "information counseling," and "assistance with difficult questions."

8. "Will accept assumption of use costs for information access comparable to present support of library activities . . ."

   They accept present cost structure (with most library costs passed through general academic fees), but they don't like being charged for searches (only a small percentage of our computerized searches are charged to users). Many have accepted costs of personal access to KI, CompuServe, etc.

221

III. FUNCTIONS OF THE ACADEMIC LIBRARIAN IN 1992

1. "Facilitators/PIGs (Professional/Personal Information Guides/Gurus)"

    We are already training users in traditional and computer oriented techniques. We provide access to esoteric materials; we provide information counseling, but could do a better job without our and users having to deal with more trivial aspects of information retrieval (e.g., how to look up a serial). We also try to keep users aware of new developments.

2. "Market Analysts . . . surveying users to determine their needs and how well we meet those needs"

    We do very little of this now. Surveying techniques would benefit from professional (non-library!) input. Good surveys of user needs would contribute much to our efforts to achieve the library of the future.

3. "Brokers . . . negotiating access to information resources, equipment and lower costs"

    We do some of this in contract negotiations, but could do more at national and regional levels.

4. "Conservators . . . identifying materials for conversion to machine-readable format"

    We currently identify materials for preservation, though usually in paper or microfilm formats. Beginning to look at digital options.

5. "Designers . . . assisting in the evaluation of existing systems, working toward improvements and developments of new systems"

    Have a lot of experience, especially in online catalogs. Very little in CD-ROMs, some in online systems. Have tended to let others design, and then we criticize the results.

6. "Reference . . . providing answers to difficult questions (Note: difficulty lies in the eyes of the requester)"

    Of course!

7. "Archivists . . . collecting, organizing and providing access to primary source and special materials . . . which may not be appropriately preserved and accessed only in digital form"

    We do this now.

8. "Developers/Producers . . . assembling and creating new information resources and databases, most likely from unique, local resources, for addition to the local/regional/national/international databases accessible through networks"

    Very little experience here, other than things like OPACs (online public access catalogs) and locally creations such as the TSDB and Jim Coble's Serials database searching software. We have Infoline, and include online versions of some of our handouts, but this is created within a set structure, inputting traditional information format.

PART THREE: HOW DO WE GET THERE?

I. THE RESOURCE BASE

1. The Plan

    More and more serials are available in full text format online, and even monographic materials and reference sets are appearing in digitized format (e.g., "Library of the Future" and several encyclopedias), but we can speed up the process by:

    - lobbying publishers to produce their materials on computers so that digital records are created

    - asking for access to those records, through subscriptions, site licenses, etc.

    - approaching present online vendors (CompuServe, Dialog, etc.) about making more of these materials available

    - targeting closed set publishers (e.g., the "Collected Works of . . .) about creating scanned databases of the publications within the set; may involve, in some instances, our contracting to do the work so that a commercial product would be created

    - working to form cooperative arrangements with publishers and libraries for creation of these databases

    - after a certain period of time (allowing for notification of publishers), refusing to add any new journal subscriptions unless we can subscribe to, or have access to, the journal databases (if an academic department is insistent on getting a title which doesn't conform, the department will have to pay for it!)

- as a corollary to the preceding point, setting a yearly goal of replacing 10% of our holdings of journal titles with digitized alternatives
- lobbying through vendors such as Yankee to get publishers to market their databases (created in the publishing process)
- identifying older, high use materials for conversion to computer-readable formats

2. The Effects
   - cost of purchasing library materials will decrease
   - cost of accessing materials will rise
   - cost of processing library materials in traditional forms (i.e., cataloging and labeling) will decrease
   - cost of processing library materials in new formats (i.e., conversion to computer-readable formats) will rise
   - ILL activity will decrease as networked access to materials increases
   - needs for quality computer equipment and network access greatly increased
   - space needs will diminish as fewer materials are added and more are converted or replaced
   - costs for memory/storage capabilities will increase, but will reflect the general decrease in per megabyte costs
   - new areas of staff activities will be:
     1. lobbying with publishers for access to materials in new formats
     2. converting materials
     3. identifying and producing new databases

II. EQUIPMENT

1. The Plan
   - the need for widely available high quality, multi-media capable computer equipment requires that the university make a major expenditure in this area; this is a crucial aspect of the plan, for

without this equipment the library of the future will never be realized

- must be in place so that replacement services are available before the services they replace are removed, in order for users to gain appropriate acceptance through experience
- must be available to the R&D staff as well, throughout the development process; will necessarily include peripherals such as scanners, software, multi-media, modems/network connections, etc.
- financing is a university responsibility, as the "product" under development is intended, ultimately, to be accessed by all members of the university community and not confined to a library building

2. The Effects

- will make the information services available to all who are connected; if it isn't an all encompassing approach, it won't work
- equipment costs very high (catch up as well as get ahead)
- costs will include not only the equipment, but will involve installation, training, maintenance and service
- cost to library as such minimal, but significant for university budget

III. ACCESS CAPABILITIES

1. The Plan

- Networking
  a. network the entire campus (complete spine)
  b. all library and information networks have to be compatible with the university network
  c. must have access to gateway services (e.g., Internet, FirstSearch, CompuServe, and America Online)
  d. charge for services through university accounts
- Front End Systems/Gateway Facilities
  a. investigate existing products (DRA, Ohio State University's system, America Online, etc.) as part of search for appropriate product

   b. definitely not a one-person project; needs to be, ultimately, developed with organization(s) with enough resources to create a system which will be widely accepted (standard!)

   c. should be seen as a learning experience, so that the system can be tried and evaluated constantly, and it should be easily modified to allow improvements as often and as soon as necessary

   d. it is not enough to have digitized data—users must be able to quickly and successfully find what they are looking for

      - an effective, intuitive front end system is crucial to the ultimate success of the system

      - will need to explore developing indexing techniques (e.g., vector/cluster/contextual analysis)

      - investigate adding fields to cataloging record (abstracts, indexes, tables of contents) as possible alternatives to LCSH (Library of Congress Subject Headings) in improving access to information; begin with a pilot project of converting Reference Collection materials' tables of contents and indexes

   e. will need staff to assist users throughout the process; role will diminish as availability of resources and effectiveness of front end systems increase

   f. will need staff for continued access to esoteric materials

2. The Effects
- will vastly improve user access to information
- will vastly reduce need for users to be in the library building
- will involve intense development efforts, but few taken by the library staff alone
- as much of the university network has been completed, and the rest is planned, this does not add any new networking costs to the university

IV. FINANCES

1. The Plan
   - users have university accounts which are directly charged, as appropriate, for accessing information resources
   - university provides financial support to users through subsidies, allocations to departmental and individual budgets, grants and in negotiating lower (group) rates and licensing fees
   - ultimately the library is out of most of the cost assessment loop
   - potential for grant support for a truly revolutionary plan

2. The Effects
   - library costs significantly lowered (effect will be especially noticeable as there is no longer a need to purchase CD-ROMs and the number of online searches plummets)
   - users cost will increase, but will directly reflect actual use, and, especially after group rate and subsidy offsets, may not vary much from current assessments for library support
   - grant support would serve to offset much of the development, acquisition, equipment and transitional costs
   - need to support outside users greatly diminished (note that the concept of the "TRLN Library" would be rendered obsolete)

V. STAFFING AND BUDGETS

1. Staffing
   - will need to be augmented through early transitional phases, but over time would be dramatically reduced
   - labor intensive aspects of present-day processing would be reduced as fewer materials come in traditional formats; staff could be redirected toward conversion projects and public service support
   - systems staff would be increased, but under the general umbrella of the university as a whole (especially for equipment and network installation and support)
   - little change in special collections staffing for some time

- administrative staff would be reduced over time (there will be fewer people to administer)

2. Budgets
   - personnel costs may rise at first, but will eventually go down
   - materials budgets for traditional formats will go down; for non-traditional formats it will rise, but over time the increase will be probably be less than if we continue in our present mode
   - costs for maintenance of present collection will diminish
   - costs for maintenance of university network and equipment will not impact on library

VI. TRADITIONS

1. "Library" will still:
   - provide assistance with special problems
   - acquire and provide access to special/esoteric materials
   - acquire and provide access to casual/recreational/avocational materials
   - hold special events (e.g., wine and cheese functions)
   - group and individual instruction (but not necessarily tied to the library building)
   - information counseling
   - study hall (though student access to the information world at their desks may reduce this need)

2. The effects of these continued services/facilities/materials are:
   - less space will be required
   - fewer staff will be required, but many will have to be technologically sophisticated, mobile and flexible
   - many tasks are ones which will already do well
   - may need special equipment for reference, instruction and counseling

APPENDIX C

THE PROGRAM PACKET

30. THE BERKELEY AGENDA

31. THE DUKE AGENDA

32. THE BUDDY PROGRAM

In this section are the separate agendas for the Berkeley and Duke Institutes and the description of the "Buddy Program." In addition to these two documents, packets included the pre-Institute assignments completed by the participants of the respective Institutes; a roster of participants (including job titles, postal addresses, e-mail addresses, and voice and fax telephone numbers), a map of the area, and a restaurant guide.

30. THE BERKELEY AGENDA

RETHINKING REFERENCE
NEW MODELS AND HOW TO GET THERE
Library Solutions Institute #2 (West)
March 12-14, 1993
The Faculty Club
University of California, Berkeley

FRIDAY

7:00-7:45pm   Registration   Seaborg Room

7:45-10:30pm
    Welcome: Anne Lipow
    Keynote: Jerry Campbell
                Aftershocks to "Shaking the Conceptual Foundations of Reference"
    Reception follows; Desserts.
    Find your buddies

SATURDAY

7:15-8:30am   Breakfast with buddies   Great Hall

8:15am   Announcements

8:45-10:00am   **Food for Thought: Case Studies**   Heyns Room

           Virginia Massey-Burzio • *Rethinking the Reference Desk: The Brandeis Experience*

           Frances Painter • *Making Tough Choices at Virginia Tech: The Pain and the Rewards*

           Janice Simmons-Welburn • *From Vision to Reality: Change at the University of Iowa*

10:00-10:30am Break

10:30-noon   **Food for Thought: Overview and Trends**
           Larry Oberg • *New Roles for "Support" Staff: Implications for Librarians*

           James Rettig • *Islands in a Sea of Change: The RQ Survey*

12:00-1:00pm   Lunch with your break-out group   Great Hall

12:30pm   Announcements

1:00-2:50pm   **Food for Thought: The Change Process**   Heyns Room

           Terry Mazany • *How the Change Process Works and how to Analyze What goes Wrong*

2:50-3:15pm   Break

3:15-5:30 pm **New Models: Brainstorming the Future**
Rethinking Reference: small group assignment: Task # 1
Lou Wetherbee, *facilitator*

SUNDAY

7:30-8:30 am Breakfast   Great Hall

8:15 am Announcements

8:45-10:30 am **Soapbox Sessions**   Heyns Room
New Reference Model(s): Analysis and Critique
Explanation of soapbox sessions: Lou Wetherbee

How will the new reference model(s)
  affect Library Administrators?   Host: Frances Painter
Reference providers   Host: James Rettig
Library users and potential users Host: Janice Simmons-Welburn
Allies, partners, and competitors Host: Suzanne Calpestri
Technical services   Host: Sue Rosenblatt
Your topic/model   Host: Volunteers welcome!!

Break refreshments will be available at buffet table throughout the soapbox sessions

10:30-11:40 am **Practical Steps: How to Get Where We Want to Go**
Small group assignment: Task # 2
Lou Wetherbee, *facilitator*

11:45-12:30 pm Small groups exchange ideas   Heyns Room

12:30-1:45 pm Lunch with your buddies   Great Hall

2:00-3:00 pm **Talkback**   Heyns Room
Anne Lipow invites participants to critique the Institute
(length, content, pacing, gains, wish-list), and to suggest next
steps, future agendas

3:00 pm Adjourn

Small Groups

Group	Room	Facilitator	Aide
A	Davis	Bill Whitson	Janice Simmons-Welbur
B	"E"	Ann Jensen	Jim Rettig
C	Louderback	Gail Schlachter	Frances Painter
D	Popper	Wendy Diamond	Ginny Massey-Burzio
E	Latimer	Jeff Pudewell	Suzanne Calpestri
F	Lewis	Myrtis Collins	Larry Oberg
G	Heyns	Ellen Meltzer	Sue Rosenblatt

231

31. THE DUKE AGENDA

RETHINKING REFERENCE
NEW MODELS AND HOW TO GET THERE
Library Solutions Institute #2 (East)
June 4-6, 1993
The Bryan Center
Duke University, Durham, North Carolina

FRIDAY

7:00-7:45 pm	Registration	Von Canon Hall
7:45-10:30 pm		

Welcome: Anne Lipow
Keynote address: Jerry Campbell
In Search of New Foundations for Reference
Reception follows; desserts and beverages
Find your buddies

SATURDAY

7:15-8:20 am	Breakfast with buddies	Von Canon A
8:10 am	Announcements	
8:30-10:30 am	**Contexts**	Von Canon C

Terry Mazany — *The Change Process: How to Make It Work*
Charles Bunge — *Vision and Values*
Suzanne Calpestri — *Allies, Partners, and Competitors*

10:35-10:55 am   Break

11am-12:25 pm   **Case Studies**

Virginia Massey-Burzio • *Eliminating the Reference Desk at Brandeis & Johns Hopkins*

Frances Painter • *Making Tough Choices at Virginia Tech; The Pain and the Rewards*

Janice Simmons-Welburn • *From Vision to Reality: Change at the University of Iowa*

Karen Williams • *Total Change at the University of Arizona*

12:30-1:45 pm   Lunch

1:00 pm   Announcements

1:55-3:00 pm   **Trends**

Larry Oberg • *New Roles for "Support" Staff: What New Roles for Librarians?*

James Rettig • *Islands in a Sea of Change: The RQ Survey*

3:00-3:20pm   Break

3:20-3:50pm   **New Directions: Brainstorming the Future**
Rethinking Reference: small group assignment: Task #1
Lou Wetherbee, *facilitator*

SUNDAY

7:15-8:30am   Breakfast   Von Canon A

8:15am   Announcements

8:45-10:30am **Soapbox Sessions**   Von Canon B & C

Explanation of soapbox sessions   Lou Wetherbee
How will the new reference model(s)
   affect Library Administrators?   Host: Frances Painter
Reference workers   Host: Jim Rettig
Library users and potential users   Host: Janice Simmons-Welburn
Allies, partners, and competitors   Host: Suzanne Calpestri
Dialogue with the advocates:
Professional values/Library education Host: Charles Bunge
Total change at the University of Arizona
                       Host: Karen Williams

Eliminating THE DESK as the
   centerpiece of reference   Host: Virginia Massey-Burzio
Support Staff/Professional Staff issues Host: Larry Oberg

Break refreshments will be available at buffet table throughout this session.

10:30-11:40   **Practical Steps: How to Get Where We Want to Go**
Small group assignment: Task #2
Lou Wetherbee, *facilitator*

11:45-12:30   Small groups exchange ideas   Von Canon C

12:30-1:45pm Lunch with your buddies   Great Hall

2:00-3:00pm   **Talkback**   Von Canon C
Anne Lipow invites participants to critique the Institute
(length, content, pacing, gains, wish-list), and to suggest next steps,
future agendas

3:00-3:30pm   Tying loose ends, for 30 minutes to adjust for other sessions that
went into overtime

3:30pm   Adjourn

32. THE BUDDY PROGRAM

BUDDY PROGRAM

Each participant in the Institute has been assigned to a small BUDDY Group. We hope that you will take advantage of this opportunity to make new friends and establish long-term professional networks.

The BUDDY idea works as follows:

On Friday evening, at the opening reception, we invite each participant to identify the BUDDIES in your group and establish contact. To assist you in locating other members of your BUDDY group, a number is printed on your name tag. The other members of your BUDDY group have the same number on their name tags. Find your BUDDIES by number and say hello.

An effort was made to form BUDDY groups of 3 or 4 participants who have at least one of the following in common:
- size of library
- level of responsibility
- subject specialty

We suggest that BUDDIES consider lunching together to share ideas and further the exchange of professional interests that we hope the entire Institute program will foster. BUDDIES may or may not be assigned to the same small working groups on Saturday afternoon and Sunday morning, so mealtimes will provide a good chance to get together.

Your BUDDIES' e-mail addresses (as well as postal and phone information) are listed in the "Participant Roster" in your packet. Following the Institute, we invite BUDDIES to stay in touch over the next year in an informal network to encourage and support each other as you create the conditions for change within your respective institutions.

33. SMALL GROUP TASK #1 AND WORKSHEETS

34. SMALL GROUP TASK #2 AND WORKSHEETS

35. SOAPBOX SESSIONS

The instructions to small groups and accompanying worksheets were prepared by Lou Wetherbee, facilitator. • *Editor*

33. SMALL GROUP TASK #1

Small Group Task #1

Identify the Components of "New Reference"

Part 1

Identify the components or characteristics of the "new reference." Based on the advance reading, the contributions of the speakers, and the ideas of your fellow participants, create a list of the key components of the new reference.

To facilitate the integration of the work of the small groups into a single document, please organize your suggestions into the following categories:

> Organizational Structure
> Staffing
> Tools & Equipment
> Services
> Clients

If you feel a category is missing, please create a separate one and identify its components. A worksheet is provided to get you started. Please use short phrases or single words to express your ideas about the components.

Part 2

Identify current components of reference service that are likely to decline in relevance and begin to disappear.

It seems likely that budgets for libraries are not going to increase significantly in the near future. In order to move to implement changes, we will have to be selective in what we do. As we go about the work of designing a new model for reference, it will be just as important to identify and eliminate or phase out unnecessary services as it will be to create or adapt alternatives. Help your small group to make some of those "hard choices".

Worksheet for Task #1, Part 1

Current Components or Characteristics of Reference:	Emerging or Desirable Components or Characteristics
Organizational Structure: • • •	Organizational Structure: • • •
Staffing: • • •	Staffing: • • •
Tools & Equipment: • • •	Tools & Equipment: • • •
Services: • • •	Services: • • •
Clients: • • •	Clients: ¥ ¥ ¥

Worksheet for Task #1, Part 2

Identify current components of reference service that are likely to decline in relevance and begin to disappear.

It seems likely that budgets for libraries are not going to increase significantly in the near future. In order to move to implement changes, we will have to be selective in what we do. As we go about the work of designing a new model for reference, it will be just as important to identify and eliminate or phase out unnecessary services as it will be to create or adapt alternatives. Help your small group to make some of those "hard choices."

Provide at least 3 suggestions. Make your suggestions in short phrases.

1.

2.

3.

34. SMALL GROUP TASK #2

Small Group Task #2

Practical Steps: How to Get Where We Want to Go

Task: Identify up to 3 specific changes which will be required to implement the new reference model(s).

For each change your group suggests, list one or two practical steps that library staff can take to implement the change.

Time: Sunday   10:30–11:40 am

Example

Change:

Reduce dependence of users on face-to-face interviews with reference librarians for commonly requested information.

Practical Steps:

- Begin a pilot program with 1 or 2 academic departments— their faculty or particular classes— that provides:
  - document delivery of electronic information
  - e-mail reference

- Develop stand-alone ready-reference micro workstations with the 100 most commonly requested pieces of information in your library, to be placed throughout the campus.

35. SOAPBOX SESSIONS

SOAPBOX SESSIONS

New Reference Model(s): Analysis and Critique

Sunday 8:45 – 9:40 am
 9:45 – 10:30 am

This is an opportunity to share your ideas about the new reference with other Institute participants. The Soapbox Sessions are informal, unrestrained discussions that do not require a specific outcome. We have designed them so that participants can learn from each other. You can move from Soapbox to Soapbox as your interests dictate. Unlike the usual round tables, you can leave one group and go to another several times where the discussion is lively.

Each Soapbox will have a volunteer "host" who will get the ball rolling. We have designated several broad areas and "hot topics" that are affected by the new reference model(s) we are creating. We invite you to question, discuss, and analyze these issues in relation to the new reference model(s).

Participants can also create new topics for discussion at one of the open Soapboxes. Flip charts will be provided at each Soapbox so that you can record ideas, illustrate points or design new organizational charts.

Refreshments will be available at a buffet table so we will not take a formal break. Get a cup of coffee and choose your topics.

Designated Soapboxes

1. Library administrators — Host: Frances Painter
2. Reference workers — Host: James Rettig
3. Library users—current and potential — Host: Janice Simmons-Welburn
4. Allies, partners, and competitors — Host: Suzanne Calpestri
5. Professional values/Library education — Host: Charles Bunge
6. Total change at the University of Arizona — Host: Karen Williams
7. Eliminating THE DESK as the centerpiece of reference — Host: Virginia Massey-Burzio
8. Support Staff/Professional Staff issues — Host: Larry Oberg
9. Your Topic/Model ? — Host: YOU ?